Read It! Play It!

with Babies and Toddlers

by
Joanne Oppenheim
and
Stephanie Oppenheim

illustrated by Joan Auclair

Designed by Joan Auclair

Musical Notation by Cathy Block and Tony Oppenheim

ISBN: 0-972105042

Oppenheim Toy Portfolio's Read It! Play It!™

Literacy Initiative continues to instill the message that reading can be a lifelong source of pleasure. **Read It! Play It! with Babies and Toddlers** is designed for making that connection to books right from the start. To help us reach as many families as possible, we are grateful to Reading Is Fundamental™, the nation's leading children's literacy organization. RIF will distribute thousands of copies of **Read It! Play It! with Babies and Toddlers** in both English and Spanish to their literacy programs across America. Reading Is Fundamental™ will also receive a $1 from every copy of the book we sell. We would also like to acknowledge the generous contribution of LeapFrog Enterprises, Inc. for their support in making the contribution to RIF possible and enabling us to reach a broader audience.

Happy Reading (and Playing!)

Joanne   *Stephanie*

Joanne and Stephanie

LeapFrog Enterprises, Inc. is proud to continue our support of the Oppenheim Toy Portfolio's Read It! Play It!™ Literacy Initiative, which promotes and enriches early learning and literacy.

As a global learning leader, LeapFrog is committed to inspiring a love of learning through our unique approach that we call LeapFrog Learning. LeapFrog creates innovative products for infants, toddlers, and preschoolers that enrich early learning experiences and fosters each child's unique abilities and interests at each appropriate developmental stage. As we develop all of our award-winning learning products, we are guided by our Educational Advisory Board, our proprietary scope and sequence for early learning, and comprehensive research in cognitive development.

At LeapFrog, every teacher and technician, every engineer and artists, everyone puts learning first. This philosophy fuels the entire company. LeapFrog knows that learning is not a part-time commitment. It requires a tremendous amount from every member of our team. We are passionately devoted to delighting and engaging children in a meaningful way by developing innovative technology-enhanced educational products. Our future is in the hands of our children and they deserve our best — every day.

Reading Is Fundamental, Inc.™ (RIF), founded in 1966, motivates children to read by working with them, their parents, and community members to make reading a fun and beneficial part of everyday life. Through its programs in every U.S. state and territory, RIF served 5 million children last year. RIF's highest priority is reaching underserved children from birth to age 8.

Grown-ups play a key role in their children's literacy development at every stage. Sharing books, playing games, singing songs, and having conversations are all great ways to give children the skills they'll need to become successful readers. RIF has developed a series of early childhood resources entitled Growing Up Reading, which can be found online at *www.rif.org/parents*. The tips found in these web materials will help you turn everyday activities into enjoyable learning experiences for babies, toddlers, and preschoolers.

For more information and to access additional reading resources, visit RIF's website at *www.rif.org*.

Reading Is Fundamental
Celebrating the Joy of Reading for 40 Years

Read It! Play It! with Babies and Toddlers

Long before babies can talk, they are able to enjoy books. For your little lap sitter, books go together with cozy time, those special moments for enjoying the warmth of your arms and the sound of your voice. To babies, books are tools for contact sport — more about being sociable than about stories. What is written on the page is less important than the pleasures of one-on-one time with the significant grown-ups in their lives. Not only do babies benefit from your undivided attention, such experiences help to develop your child's long-lasting and positive attitudes about the delights found in books and reading.

Sharing books, talking, and singing with little ones is also an important way to foster their language development. Studies show that babies who are talked to from the start have 300 more words in their vocabulary at age two than children who do not have adults who communicate with them. Just hearing language on TV or grown-ups talking to each other doesn't do the trick. One-on-one interactions between babies and their caregivers are key to developing the brain and language skills. Reciting rhymes as you move baby's arms and legs; singing songs as you carry her about; playing clap and bounce lap trots are all fun ways to surround your child with meaningful language.

As you change your baby's clothes, drive to the store, or give a bath, telling little stories about what you are doing makes a fine story for beginners. All through the early years, everyday events make good raw material for story-time. These stories are not in any book, but in your head. "Tell me about the time when I...." stories are likely to become cherished family stories as time goes on. But for beginners, simply describing what you are doing often leads to give and take "dialogue." Listen to your baby's babble and respond to her baby talk. Long before they can talk with words, babies will respond if you engage them in "conversation." Copy the faces your baby makes. If she sticks out her tongue, you do it, too. If she sneezes, you sneeze. If she hiccups, hiccup back.

These face-to-face, eye-to-eye, heart-to-heart interchanges are key to language development. We are the only species that must learn our language. A dog will bark and a kitten will meow instinctively, even if they do not hear another dog or cat. But human babies must hear their language if they are to speak. Hundreds of years ago Frederick the Great tried to discover what language babies would speak instinctively. He ordered the caregivers in an orphanage not to speak to the babies, in hopes of solving the mystery. But, the babies in those silent rooms never spoke! Without the give and take of dialogue the children never learned to speak.

Using This Book

Making the most of early book experiences can be good fun. We'll give you strategies and games to play that will enlarge the fun and learning. You will also find songs, rhymes, and playful activities that will extend the books. Keep in mind that for young children such activities are about exploring materials rather than producing end products. As they do so, you can enlarge the experience just as you enlarge upon their first short "sentences." When your two-year-old points and says "Wow! Wow!" you are likely to agree and add, "Yes, what a big black doggie!" Similarly, when your child is unable to describe feelings in words, but conveys fears or delight with body language, you read her meaning and may even express those feelings back to her.

You'll find the books arranged in age order with books and activities for littlest listeners followed by books for older toddlers. Keep in mind that many of the baby books continue to be of interest although the games may become more complex as your child grows from lap baby to get about child. We have selected books that you will find with ease in libraries and bookstores.

Although most of us think of books as a part of the bedtime ritual, reading to your baby and toddler need not be reserved for the end of the day. Keep books handy to share during transition times when the tempo of the day needs changing. Keep a book in the diaper bag you carry on visits to Grandma's or the pediatrician's waiting room. Clear a low shelf where toddlers can help themselves to books independently. Just as we nourish their growing bodies with good food, these early book experiences on your lap are fundamental to nourishing their minds and a lifetime love of reading.

Why These Books?

Some of the titles we've included are classics, such as *Goodnight Moon, The Runaway Bunny,* and *Caps for Sale.* You may remember some of these books from your own childhood. They have stood the test of time, and should be enjoyed by a new generation of readers. There are other new titles that are developmentally appropriate for the youngest reader. You may notice that some other traditional picture books are missing, such as *The Three Little Pigs* or *Where the Wild Things Are.* Babies and toddlers are not ready for long plot lines or potentially scary imaginary creatures.

Many of the techniques used with these books can be used with other books, as well. Finding playful ways to extend the fun is key to building your child's love of books and reading.

TABLE OF CONTENTS

FIRST LITTLE STORIES AND CONCEPT BOOKS

Knowing and Naming Books

Before they are ready for "once upon a time" stories, babies see books as amazing objects to be explored with all the senses. Watch how seriously they work at turning the pages and exploring the images. Indeed, to babies and toddlers, a book is a mechanical wonder, with pages to be turned, touched, tossed, and sometimes even torn! Choose sturdy cloth and cardboard books for this "search and destroy" stage.

These "knowing and naming" books represent an important intellectual milestone for infants. A few years from now your child will learn that the letters **c-u-p** stand for something we drink from. The word "cup" is a symbol for that object; one that makes a picture in your mind when you read it, even if a photo is not there. But for babies, recognizing an object from a photo is a first step in learning to read symbols. The ability to understand that one thing can stand for another is no small thing. Looking at a photo of a cup on a page, your baby is "reading" a representation of the real thing.

For beginners it is important to choose books with photos or clear illustrations that are easy to recognize. Save the arty images for older children who have clear and firm images of familiar objects. Keep in mind that to your baby there are many new things to learn about. It is no small feat for toddlers to understand that the family pooch is not only known as Prince, but it is also called a doggie. Furthermore, it takes time and repeated conversations to learn that all four-legged furry animals are not necessarily named Prince, nor are they all dogs!

1

For young children, steer clear of fantasy or cartoonish illustrations. One teacher remembers a preschooler who returned day after day to a book of Dr. Seuss' fantastic animal creations. The look on his face made it clear that the pictures were more worrisome than pleasing. Finally he asked the teacher where these weird-looking creatures lived. This was a three-year-old who was working on recognizing farm animals, zoo animals, and pet animals. Suddenly, he was afraid of where or when he might meet some of these imaginary creatures. Babies and toddlers need to sort out the real world before they move on to fantasy.

A few words of caution: Check the corners and edges of books and especially the flaps of die-cut pages. These are often sharp and can do damage to little hands and faces. Much as we like the idea of touchy-feely books, which match baby's sensory way of learning, all too often these have pull-off parts and fuzz, which present a choking hazard. Books with wheels, buttons, and other doo-dads are not for children under three, although the warning labels are often in fine print or missing. Remember, babies and toddlers don't just listen to books, they experience them with all their senses — they taste and teethe on them, too.

First Books for Babies & Young Toddlers

Read It!

Spot's Favorite Words

(by Eric Hill, Putnam) Use this chunky little book to talk about the familiar objects on the pages. Every pair of pages includes an easy-to-identify object that is shown in isolation and in context. Designed with small pages that fit easily in little hands, this is sure to be among your baby's favorite first books. Also look for other "knowing and naming" books that feature Maisy, a popular storybook character by Lucy Cousins. See **Maisy's Favorite Animals, Clothes, Toys,** and **Things** (Candlewick).

Play It!

Smart Baby Knowing & Naming Games Language

First picture books may have no more than one word, or even no words at all. The "story" you will tell is not on the printed page, but in your head, and likely to change each time you "read" it.

- One day you may talk about the sippy cup on the page, saying, "Oh, look, a red cup just like yours!"

- On another reading, you might say, "M-m-m-m, I'm thirsty! I wonder if there is milk in the cup?"

- And on yet another reading, you might say, "A cup for juice! O-o-o, look at the duck on the cup!"

- Pretend to pick the cup off of the page, put it to your mouth and make drinking sounds! Ham it up!

Tips for choosing other knowing and naming books . . .

1. Art should be photos or realistic and easy-to-identify illustrations.

2. Avoid cluttered pages for now. One clear image per page is enough for beginners.

3. Select books with familiar items. Knowing and naming a dog comes before an armadillo or an albatross.

WHAT THEY LEARN. Knowing and naming books help develop language.

Tracking Games

Following a moving object is no small feat for the new baby. Use a boldly patterned soft toy with quiet rattle or squeaky sound to get baby's attention. Give it a shake and move it slowly from side to side in baby's line of vision. In time baby will reach out to touch, but for starters, looking and listening is the name of the game. Remember, newborns can't focus on objects more than 8–14 inches from their eyes.

Read It!

Ten Little Fingers

(by Annie Kubler, Child's Play) Delightful babies go through the motions of this favorite rhyme. Read it for the sound, play it with your baby for the fun. At first you will do the actions, but before long your baby will be doing the motions. Kubler's jolly baby illustrations are charming. This and other familar nursery rhymes are ideal for one-on-one playtime.

Play It!

Pat-a-Cake   **Active Play/Socializing**

Whether your baby is flat on his back or sitting up, this is a favorite. Take baby's hands in yours and clap as you say:

> Pat-a-cake, pat-a-cake, Baker man
> Bake me a cake as fast as you can!
> Roll it up *[roll baby's arms]* and roll it up
> And mark it with a B *[trace a B on baby's tummy]*
> And put it in the oven *[Put baby's arms over head]*
> For baby and me!

Other action games will help babies discover their hands and feet as well as enjoy being social. Having a few such games up your sleeve can turn a cranky moment into a playful one. Quick little games work well when getting changed is taking too long, or you are in a hold-and-wait situation.

Everything That Goes Up

Here's a little baby science lesson. Hold your hand up in the air in baby's sight line, saying:

>> Everything that goes up comes down, down, down!

Gradually spiral your hand down, down, down, gently tickling baby on the tummy. Before long baby will anticipate the tickles, and giggle before your fingers touch!

Buzzing Bees

Babies love the surprise action and sound of this little hand game, which involves listening, watching, and feeling.

Here is the beehive. *[hold your fist up in the air]*
Where are the bees? *[keep fist closed]*
They're hiding inside — do you want to see?
One, two, three . . .
[pop 1, 2, 3 fingers out]
B-z-z-z-z-z-z-z! *[Buzz your hand down to tickle baby's tummy]*

WHAT THEY LEARN. Tracking games develop baby's visual perception as they gain the ability focus and follow for longer periods of time. It's important to "read" baby's readiness, as well as signals that he's tired or needs a break, as he looks away.

7

Read It!

My First Real Mother Goose

(illus. by Blanche Fisher Wright, Scholastic) Familiar rhymes such as "Jack and Jill," "Baa, Baa, Black Sheep," and "Ring Around the Rosie" are in this sturdy board book. These have a classic look. For a gentler, sweeter board book collection, see **Tomie's Little Mother Goose** (Tomie dePaola, Putnam). Either makes a good choice for beginners.

Play It!

Action Games	Active Play/Language/Socializing

This Little Piggy Went to Market

This little piggy went to market
[touch baby's thumb]
This little piggy stayed home
[touch baby's pointer finger]
This little piggy had roast beef
[touch baby's middle finger]
This little piggy had none
[touch baby's ring finger]
This little piggy cried, "Wee, wee, wee!" all the way home!
[run your fingers from baby's foot or hand up her body to her tummy and tickle her under her chin. Play this with the other hand, and then the toesies.]

Humpty Dumpty

Humpty Dumpty sat on a wall.
[Hold your sitting-up baby on your lap facing you]
Humpty Dumpty had a great fall.
    [Hold baby and shake your knees, gently pushing baby down on her back]
    All the King's horses and all the King's men . . .
    [Wiggle your fingers as if they were king's men on horses trotting on baby's tummy]
    . . .couldn't put Humpty together again!

Ride a Cock Horse

[Bounce baby gently on your knee as you say this rhyme.]
Ride a cock horse to Banbury Cross
To see a great lady upon a white horse.
Rings on her fingers, and bells on her toes,
She shall have music wherever she goes!

WHAT THEY LEARN. Babies and toddlers enjoy the rhythm of Mother Goose rhymes and the fun of playful interactions with their caregivers. For toddlers, combining words with actions gives concrete meaning to the words. These little rhymes are part of the literary landscape of childhood.

9

Read It!

Peekaboo Kisses

(by Barney Salzberg, Harcourt) Baby's favorite game is played again and again in this "touch and feel" book. Each of the animals has a texture to feel after you flip the pages open to a new peek-a-boo. There's a small squeaky mouse and a final page with a mirror that reflects you know who! Available in Spanish. Also, a similar idea but with realistic photos of babies and toys, **Playtime Peekaboo!** (DK).

Play It!

Ways to Peek-a-Boo   Active Play/Self Image

Few games have more appeal than variations of peek-a-boo. Playing little games in which you (or an object) appear and disappear can't really be understood until little ones begin to comprehend that *out of sight* is not *out of existence*. Psychologists call this "object permanence" — something babies really "get" at about 8 months old. Try it with a younger baby and you are not likely to get much response. Try it again a few months later and it is likely to spark repeated giggles. For toddlers, the classic hands-over-face game is old hat, but variations of peek-a-boo remain great fun.

Baby Peek-a-Boo Games

• Put your hands over your face and ask, "Where's Mommy?" Pull hands away and say, "Peek-a-boo!" If baby seems too startled or alarmed, try the game again in a few weeks. Your reappearance should spark a smile, not alarm.

• Play little games of peek-a-boo as you reveal your smiling face from behind a book, door, or piece of furniture. Or put a napkin over your face and ask, "Where's Daddy?" Baby will love pulling the cloth away and finding you! Older babies will like reversing roles. Put the napkin on baby's face and she will pull it away and giggle when you say "Peek-a-boo!"

- Hide a musical toy under a pillow. Ask your baby if she can find the musical toy. Using the sound to hone in on the object calls for another kind of attention.

Who's That?

Your baby in arms will be amazed to catch sight of herself and you in a mirror. Watch her surprise as she sees you twice — the real you and your reflection. Talk about what she sees and let her touch your face and your reflection. Move baby in and out of the sight line of the mirror, playing yet another variation of Peek-a-Boo!

WHAT THEY LEARN. Peek-a-boo is a reassuring game that lets children solve a small mystery with success and feel empowered by their cleverness.

Read It!

Counting Kisses

(by Karen Katz, Little Simon) How many kisses to say goodnight? This little counting book is not so much about numbers as it is about getting cozy and ready for sleep. It is likely to become part of your young toddler's must-have bedtime favorites, especially if you serve up the kisses. Start with "ten little kisses on teeny tiny toes" and count down from there. A bedtime valentine!

Play It!

Sweet Dreams   Establishing Your Own Bedtime Rituals

It's fair to say that getting baby to sleep can sometimes be the most challenging time of the day or night. You are tired, the baby is tired, and you want the day to end on a pleasant note. Ideally you will make going to bed into a predictable series of low-key but soothing events. A not-too-exciting tub time, followed by a book or two will often calm a tired baby down. Little laptime games, such as fingerplays coupled with lullabies, are perfect for this part of the day.

Babies are not bored by doing or hearing the same things again and again. In fact it helps them predict what comes next and provides the comfort of knowing and feeling safe. Whether you rock your baby in your arms or put her into the crib, a good-night lullaby or two can also work the magic trick that carries them off to dreamland.

Songs that you recall from your own childhood are ideal. Your baby may respond to a classic such as Brahms' "Lullaby," or you may prefer a folk tune such as "Hush, Little Baby."

Having a few songs in your nightly repertoire is most useful.

Hush, Little Baby

Hush, little baby, don't say a word,
Papa's [Mama's] gonna buy you a
  mockingbird.
And if that mockingbird won't sing,
Papa's gonna buy you a diamond ring
And if that diamond ring turns brass,
Papa's gonna buy you a looking glass

And if that looking glass gets broke,
Papa's gonna buy you a billy goat.
And if that billy goat won't pull,
Papa's gonna buy you a cart and bull.
And if that cart and bull fall down,
You'll still be the sweetest little baby
  in town.

Read It!

The Itsy-Bitsy Spider

(by Rosemary Wells, Scholastic) You can play this classic rhyme with your baby as a tickling game and then play it as a fingerplay game as your baby grows into a toddler. For starters, use this little book to sing the rhyme. Sing it again while you dress baby after a bath. Having some playful rhymes and songs to sing as you dress baby can make the whole process happier.

Play It!

Itsy-Bitsy Spider   Tickle Game

The itsy bitsy spider went up the water spout
[creep your fingers up baby's legs and tummy]
Down came the rain and washed the spider out
[wiggle your fingers over baby's head down to his body]
Out came the sunshine and dried up all the rain
[Make a big arc with your hands to show the sun coming out]
And the itsy bitsy spider went up the spout again!
[creep your fingers up baby's legs and tummy and tickle baby under the chin]

Older toddlers will like doing this fingerplay by following your lead...

The itsy bitsy spider went up the waterspout
[Use fingers to make spider walk up]

Down came the rain and washed the spider out
[Use fingers to show rain falling down]
Out came the sunshine and dried up all the rain
[Hold hands up in air as if holding the big sun]
And the itsy bitsy spider went up the spout again.
[Use fingers to make spider walk up again]

*Some people say "itsy-bitsy," others say "eency-weency."

The een cy wen cy spi der went up the wa ter spout   Down came the rain

and washed the spi der out!   Out came the sun   and dried up all the rain

And   the een   cy wen   cy spi   der   went up   the spout   a gain!

WHAT THEY LEARN. Babies and toddlers learn a lot about predicting what happens next as you play this game with them. It is a sequence of events that they soon remember and enjoy playing again and again, because they remember.

Read It!

All Fall Down

(by Helen Oxenbury, Simon & Schuster)
Adorable babies are pictured playing typical
baby day games. The simple text is rhythmic
and appealing to babies and toddlers. One of
several charming books in a series by Helen
Oxenbury.

Play It!

Dance with Me!   **Active Play/Music**

Before baby can get up and boogie on his two feet, he'll enjoy moving about
in your arms. Depending on the mood, try some slow, soothing dancing. Or
for livelier moments, go on and rock and roll that baby. It's a great way to
release your tension as well as baby's.

Ring Around a Rosy

Somewhere between 8 and 12 months, most babies learn to pull
themselves upright. Before baby can stand alone, she
loves standing up while holding on to your hands.
When baby pulls up, sing "Ring Around A Rosy."
Baby will enjoy "dancing" to this little rhyme and
anticipate the falling down action! Older tots, who
can really stand up, will like to dance in a circle and
then fall down with you.

Ring Around a Rosy
A pocket full of posies
Ashes, ashes! We all fall down!

Pop! Goes the Weasel

What's the opposite of "we all fall down"?
Play this for reverse action: start with a
sitting-down baby and clap baby's
hands as you sing:

All around the cobbler's bench
The monkey chased the weasel.
The monkey thought 'twas all in fun . . .
Pop! goes the weasel! *(Lift baby up when you sing "Pop!")*

Smart Baby Tricks

Light Up the Sky!

Talk about making things happen — lift baby
up and let him switch the lights on and off as
you enter a room. What magic!

WHAT THEY LEARN. These
active games develop memory
through repetition. In time, baby
will initiate the games by giving
you her hands, or with other
non-verbal signals that say she
wants to . . . play it again, Sam!

Read It!

Good Morning, Baby!

(by Jo Foord, et al., DK) Babies love to see other babies doing the things they do. With colorful photos this book follows babies, from infants to toddlers, through the day. A companion book, **Good Night, Baby!** covers the bedtime ritual. These are good talking books for telling your own stories. Available in Spanish. Also, for a charming good start to the day, see **Peekaboo Morning** (by Rachel Isadora, Putnam).

Play It!

How Big?

Here's a good game for changing table time. While baby is flat on his back, say, "How big is the baby?" Take baby's hands in yours and lift his arms up over his head and say, "SOOO Big!" At first you'll do all the action, but before long, when you ask, "How big is baby?" he'll lift his arms and happily do this smart baby trick!

Your Own Baby's Stories   Socializing

Some of the best stories are the ones you tell as you feed your baby breakfast and talk about the m-m-m-m smooth oatmeal that you "stir, stir, stir" 'til it is just right. You don't need pictures or words in a book. The action and story are right there where you are. Use your baby's name: "I'm fixing and mixing

Jake's oatmeal. M-m-m-m-m, this is going to be so good! Jake's little spoon is going 'round and 'round . . . now, let's have a taste!" Oh, oh! when a little fist gets into the cereal, talk about how the "icky sticky oatmeal" feels!

Road Trips

In the car, you may be driving, but there's no reason to travel in silence. Talk about where you are going and what you are seeing along the way. Every trip is full of starts and stops and sights and sounds. Of course, you can't talk endlessly, but as the narrator of events you have an important role in explaining the world of things. These monologues soon become dialogues. At first, you will get some two-way babble that's well worth listening to. Give it a few more months, and single words and phrases will follow.

Two-Way Games   Active Play
Pull a Toy

Put a toy that's out of baby's reach on a scarf or towel that baby can reach. Can baby figure out how to get the toy by pulling the scarf to him? Demo the action and then try again.

WHAT THEY LEARN. These are games that develop baby's sense of "can do" — a first step toward independence, even before they can walk or talk.

Read It!

I Like It When...

(by Mary Murphy, Harcourt) A penguin chick and a big penguin enjoy each other's company doing everyday things. Each turn of the page reinforces the warm relationship between these two. This can be enjoyed by parent and child or caregiver and child. Either way, it reflects a toddler's world and the happy moments.

Play It!

Two-Way Games   **Socializing**

Drop It!

Your baby keeps dropping spoons, bread, toys, cup, whatever off the high chair table. This is more than a way to give parents exercise. Remember, just a few weeks ago objects were dropped only accidentally. Now, baby can voluntarily release things from his hands. It's also a great way to learn more about cause and effect.

Give & Take

Once baby can release objects at will from her hands, she will enjoy little give-and-take games. Just don't tease! Ask baby to give you a specific toy. Say thanks and give it back to her. It's a new twist on taking turns that baby can enjoy again and again. Remember, repetition is fun to baby.

20

Roly Poly Ball

There is no better basic toy than a soft fabric ball and the simple games you can play together. Your sitting-up and crawling baby will love the back-and-forth fun of rolling a ball. Choose a soft fabric ball with jingle inside, or a big beach ball that's slightly soft.

Roly Poly I

Even before your sitting-up baby can crawl, play a roly poly game. Sit close to baby with legs outstretched. Simply roll the ball between you and baby.

Roly Poly II

Once baby begins crawling about, that ball will be a favorite plaything for chasing games. Stick to the fabric ball, which is easier for little hands to grasp and toss.

WHAT THEY LEARN.
These games are a great way to introduce active physical play that both is social and develops big motor skills.

Read It!

I Can

(by Helen Oxenbury, Candlewick) Delicious illustrations of toddlers on the go. Like toddlers, this is all about locomotion of the personal kind . . . toddlers running, jumping, kicking, sliding. Also in the same series: *I Touch* and *I See*. These titles have been scaled down into a mini-board book set, but we prefer the full-size look and feel of original individual books.

Play It!

Make an "I Can" Book   **Self Image**

Use duplicate photos of your baby doing active things for a small photo album.

Label the photos with the action words that describe what is happening. For example, "Emily eating," "Emily climbing," "Emily drinking," "Emily reading," "Emily bathing," etc.

This is sure to become a family treasure, not to mention a toddler "I Can Do It" favorite right now.

WHAT THEY LEARN. Homemade books not only add to a child's library, but these books can also be personalized to include the child and his special likes and interests.

More Smart Baby "I Can Do That!" Tricks

Waving Bye-Bye and Throwing Kisses.

When someone leaves, baby can't say goodbye. But with a little encouragement, she will delight in waving bye-bye or throwing kisses — except when you want him to do it.

Knock It Off. Baby often pulls up in the crib and sidesteps about. Learning to let go and stay standing takes practice. Try this little game: Put a soft toy on the crib rail to encourage your baby to side step and knock it off the rail. This game is fun for older sibs who don't mind playing pick-up.

Booom!

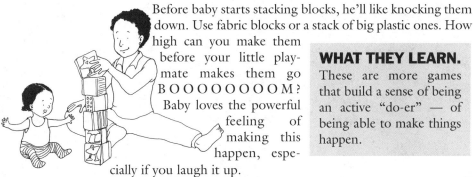

Before baby starts stacking blocks, he'll like knocking them down. Use fabric blocks or a stack of big plastic ones. How high can you make them before your little play-mate makes them go B O O O O O O O O M? Baby loves the powerful feeling of making this happen, especially if you laugh it up.

WHAT THEY LEARN. These are more games that build a sense of being an active "do-er" — of being able to make things happen.

23

Read It!

Wheels On the Bus

(by Raffi/illus. by Sylvie Wickstrom, Crown) There are many versions of this classic song. One of our favorites is the Paul Zelinsky pop-up version (Dutton), which is amazing but easy to rip. You may want to bring that book home and share it only for lap time with supervision. Raffi's board book edition feels and looks sturdy enough to make the journey. This ever-popular song is fun to sing to your baby with body motions. Make them up or check out our suggestions below.

Play It!

Go for a Spin Game　　　**Dramatic play/music**

The wheels on the bus go round and round
[gently move baby's legs like a bike]
Round and round
Wheels on the bus go round and round
All through the town.

The doors on the bus go open and shut
[clap baby's hands together]
Open and shut, open and shut . . .

The people on the bus go up and down
[gently sit or stand baby up and down]
Up and down, up and down . . .

The driver on the bus says "Move on back!
[move one of baby's arms up and down]
Move on back, move on back!" ...

The wipers on the bus go swish, swish, swish
[move baby's arms from side to side]
Swish, swish, swish. Swish, swish, swish ...

Toddler Variations: Older tots who are beyond your moving their arms and legs will enjoy following your motions as they act out this classic song. You can add as many actions and variations as you like to keep those wheels rolling!

Wheels go round and round *[turn arms and hands in circles]*

Doors open and shut *[clap hands together]*

Driver says move on back
[motion hand over shoulder]

Wipers go swish *[hands back and forth from side to side]*

People go up and down
[stand up and sit down]

WHAT THEY LEARN.
Associating words with actions gives meaning to those words.

Read It!

Touch and Feel Home

(DK books) This is one in a series of sturdy cardboard books with textures for baby to feel. Babies do learn a lot through all their senses and touchy-feely books give you a chance to talk about different textures — smooth, bumpy, furry, soft, and hard — to name but a few. This book tours the home, with familiar objects to explore and talk about. There are many books of this kind in the bookstores, but some have doo-dads that are easy to pull off and may become a choking hazard. Look at such books with care and steer clear of feathers and long haired furry trims. Available in Spanish.

Play It!

First Toys   **Sensory Learning**

When you select toys for your baby you'll want to provide a variety of props for sensory learning. Soft toys with differing sounds, textures, and patterns match your baby's style of learning. He'll use all his senses to explore his world. He feels them with his little hands and feet, he examines them with his eyes and fingers, he tastes them with his mouth and listens to them with his ears. All of these sensory experiences are part of his learning experiences. Talking about the wet water in the tub, the loud sound of a spoon hitting a metal pot, the silky feel of a satin binding on a blankie, enlarges his hands-on discoveries.

Look for opportunities to talk about the feel and sounds of everyday experiences . . . the mushy feel of a banana, the crunchy sound of a cracker, the cold feel of snow. You don't need to quiz him on these words, just use them in the course of enlarging upon his discoveries.

Make an "I Touch" Book

Make your own library of touchy-feely books for baby to explore.

- You can stitch together a washable texture book with a variety of fabric scraps and talk about how they feel. Use squares of corduroy, terrycloth, satin, cotton, velvet or velour.

- Or glue a variety of textures onto construction paper pages and lace the binding of the book with a satiny ribbon. You might use bumpy paper from a cookie box, a piece of bubble wrap, a square of foil, a patch of sand paper. This kind of book needs to be checked to be sure it is holding together.

Read It!

Baby Talk

(by Dawn Sirett/photos by Victoria Blackie, DK) Babies love photos of babies and they will especially love the playful peek-a-boo experience as they look at the baby on the left page and then see a close-up of the same baby under the flap. This sturdy construction of the book will withstand repeat explorations.

1 2 3 bebé/Baby 123

(DK) This bilingual book is not so much about counting as it is about the things babies do, including crawling, eating and playing. As your baby becomes more interested in numbers, you can use it for simple counting games.

Play It!

What Does Baby Say?   Language

Before you open the flaps page in *Baby Talk*, you can ask, "What's the baby doing?" Talk about what the baby is saying on each page as you lift the flap. Before long, your baby is likely to be saying many of the same sounds.

What Does Baby Do?

As you look at the pages of babies playing, talk about the baby who is clapping her hands or reading a book. Talk about the babies who are taking a bath. "Can you find the baby who is holding his foot? Where is your foot?" You don't need to turn this into a quiz, but rather talk about the details as you look at the babies on each page. In asking questions, you are doing most of the talking. Gradually your questions will prompt your child's use of words. Use this as an opportunity to enlarge upon what he says.

What's Inside?

Put five or six interesting small toys and baby books in a paper bag or box for baby to pull out and explore. A fun way to help baby establish short independent playtimes. Small boxes with toys inside motivate exploration and make happy surprises. At this stage, babies are happy just to take things out. Their focus is on the "dumping" end of the filling-and-dumping game. Filling comes later, we promise.

Active Floor Games

I'll Catch You & You Catch Me! Get down on the floor and take turns playing a crawling catch game. Say, "I'm going to catch you!" and crawl after baby. Or play it in reverse, telling baby to "Try and catch me!" Go slowly enough so baby can catch you. This can be a pretty exciting game!

WHAT THEY LEARN. These first social games give baby a sense of joy in your company. Taking time to laugh and play together can be as refreshing to you and your little one.

Read It!

Where is Baby's Belly Button?

(by Karen Katz, Little Simon) Lift the flaps and find baby's eyes under a hat; baby's mouth behind the cup; baby's hands under the bubbles and other peek-a-boo surprises. Babies love playing peek-a-boo and learning the names of the parts of their bodies.

Play It!

Where is My Baby's Belly Button?   Knowing & Naming Game

After reading this book, play a game of finding your baby's pretty eyes, chubby hands, little feet, and tickly bellybutton. For beginners, you'll be asking the questions and answering them, too.

Ask: "Where are baby's hands?"
Answer: "I see baby's hands!" (clap them gently)

Ask: "Where are baby's feet?"
Answer: "I see baby's feet!" (touch baby's toes)

Ask: "Where is baby's belly button?"
Answer: "I see baby's belly button!" (give baby a zerbert)

Before long baby will be giving you his hands, showing you his ears, eyes, and picking up his shirt for a tickly zerbert! Use any excuse to give your baby a wet zerbert kiss. Puff your lips and let it rip!

Variation: As babies grow into toddlers, add other body-part words to the list . . . fingers, neck, chin, hair, elbow, knees, etc.

Two-Way Knowing & Naming Game

Of course, your baby often examines your face, touching your nose, pulling your hair, putting little fingers to your lips. It's almost as if baby is asking for some naming and knowing games. For starters you can say "Mommy's nose" (wiggle it) . . . "Here's baby's nose!" (touch it).

As knowing and naming becomes more of a game, asking baby to show you her nose, her mouth, her pretty eyes becomes a great baby trick they like to perform.

WHAT THEY LEARN.

Knowing, naming, and finding the parts of their faces and other body parts is no small task. Vary the choices to match your child — for example, with a two year old, you'll sing about arms and legs, but with a four and five you'll get on to details such as shoulder, knee, and ankle.

Games to Sing   Language/Self Awareness

Play as you sing to the tune of "A Hunting We Will Go":

Oh, where is (child's name)'s nose?
Oh where is _____'s nose?
Hi ho the cherry oh!
I see _____'s nose!
[Substitute other body parts as you sing this again.]

Oh where is (child's name)'s nose? Oh where is _____'s nose?

Hi ho the cher ry oh! I see_____ _____'s nose!

Read It!

Bubbles, Bubbles

(by Kathi Appelt/illus. Fumi Kosaka, HarperFestival) Here is a bubblicious ode to sudsy tubs and bath time! Oh, if only it were this easy! Using playful language — "splashy, splashy, splooshy, scrubbles" — this is a slice-of-life tale about a toddler who needs a tub. If you prefer your tub tale to be once removed, share *Mrs. Wishy-Washy* (by Joy Crowley, Philomel), in which each of the muddy animals gets clean until they go back outside and dive back into the mud!

Play It!

Baby Bath Game	Music / Tub Fun

Knowing and naming body parts is more fun when you sing them. Change the words to "This is the Way We Wash Our Clothes" to a bathe-the-baby song:

> This is the way we wash your toes
> Wash your toes, wash your toes
> This is the way we wash your toes
> Rub-a-dub-dub in the tub!

Variations: Substitute toes with hands, elbows, legs, tummy, etc. As language grows, so can the range of body parts, to include neck, shoulder, knees . . .

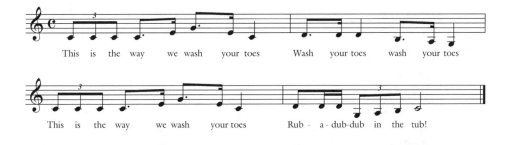

This is the way we wash your toes Wash your toes wash your toes

This is the way we wash your toes Rub - a - dub-dub in the tub!

Bubbles, Bubbles Everywhere

Long before babies can wave a wand or blow bubbles, they will enjoy watching them. Bring a bottle of bubble solution outside and give it a try. Even a horizontal baby will enjoy watching the bubbles drift on a breeze. Young toddlers may not be able to make the bubbles, but chasing them fits right into their active on-the-go style.

Wash the Dishes Game

Wash the dishes *[rub baby's hands together]*
Wipe the dishes *[keep rubbing hands]*
Ring the bell for tea *[shake hands back and forth]*
Three good wishes *[roll baby's legs]*
Three good kisses *[kiss baby's tummy]*
I will give to thee!

WHAT THEY LEARN. More playful ways to know and name the parts of the body and enjoy the important routines of hygiene.

Read It!

Baby Colors / Los colores del bebé

(DK) There are many objects of the same color on each of the two page spreads. Cute babies are surrounded by clear photos of things that are all the same color. Some are less familiar than others. Fun for pointing and talking about. A bilingual book in English and Spanish. Also suggested, **Colores** (DK) has handsome photos with fewer objects on each page for the younger baby to explore.

My Colors / Mis Colores

(by Rebecca Emberly. Little, Brown) Color books such as this one tend to be more abstract. The big red apple is easy to recognize, but to a baby the yellow sun may be more puzzling. For the young baby photos are a better choice. These and other books in Rebeccca Emberly's bilingual series, however, have beautiful images and make a good transition for older babies and toddlers.

Play It!

Playing With Colors   **Language**

Learning color names is not something you need to drill your baby on. The books here are more about knowing and naming things than they are about color. They focus on color as another way of looking at the world of things. If you use color words in their everyday experiences they will know their colors without the need for quizzing.

As you dress your baby, you can use colors to talk about . . .

"Look, today you are wearing your red socks."

When you open a banana you can talk about . . .
"M-m-m, what a big yellow banana!"

If you are in the grocery you can talk about . . .
"My, what nice orange oranges!

Similarly, when baby is playing with toys, you can talk about the color of the blocks, balls, or toy cars. Knowing color names comes gradually and naturally if you use the words or enlarge upon what they say. When baby says "Cup," enlarge upon it by saying "Your nice blue cup."

WHAT THEY LEARN. Opportunities to learn color names are everywhere and they are learned best through real-life experiences.

Read It!

Happy Baby Animals

(by Roger Priddy, Priddy Books) Realistic photographs of animals are sorted by their habitat in this sturdy board book. This is chock-full of animals you'll find on the farm, in the zoo, in the woods and the jungle. Young babies will enjoy this best if you provide some sound effects as you go. Later on it will be fun to use for "I spy" riddle games.

Play It!

More Knowing and Naming   **Language**

Babies are keenly aware of the animals in their world. Many baby books include animals that are pretty far from the familiar dog, cat, and bird they see and the illustrations often add to the confusion. We suggest clear photos of familiar animals as a better choice. When you take a walk or a ride, be sure to talk about the animals you see along the way. Point out the dogs, squirrels, and pigeons you spot in the park. Watch for cows and horses on the roadside as you go driving. It takes a while before toddlers have the names of four-legged animals pinned down.

First Books for Babies & Young Toddlers

Pony Trot — Bouncing Game

Sitting-up babies like this knee bouncing game. Bounce gently as you say this rhyme . . .

> This is the way the pony trots
> Trip, trot, trip, trot
> This is the way the pony trots
> Trip, trot,trip, trot . . . STOP!
> *[Stop the motion, lower your knee, and hold baby as he slides down]*

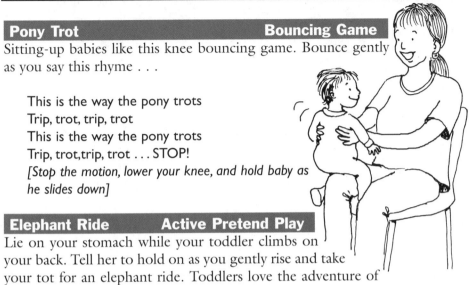

Elephant Ride — Active Pretend Play

Lie on your stomach while your toddler climbs on your back. Tell her to hold on as you gently rise and take your tot for an elephant ride. Toddlers love the adventure of riding about as you lumber along on the floor. It's a kind of gentle rough-housing that leads to lots of giggles and, we hope, not a backache. This is for older toddlers who can hang on.

Variation: **Piggyback.** Riding on your shoulders, your tot gets a bird's-eye view of the world.

WHAT THEY LEARN. Recognizing animals is basic to knowing and naming the world your child lives in.

First Little Stories & Concept Books

Perhaps the first true storybook most children hear is Margaret Wise Brown's classic *Goodnight Moon*. In many ways, this is more like a knowing and naming book that is set in nightly ritual of saying good night. Its rhyming cadence makes it as soothing as a lullaby, which toddlers soon know by heart. It's easy for children to identify with the little bunny, who is like a child in "fur clothing." Keep the simplicity of the storyline in mind as you select other books for young listeners. Toddlers enjoy small stories that reflect the routines of their day. Steer clear of long and complex story lines.

Many preschool picture books that are more appropriate for older children are now being produced in cardboard editions. This makes them look like books for babies and toddlers. Is there really a difference? Yes, indeed! Read the stories and look at the pictures. Toddlers live very much in the here and now. There is much to learn about real people, places, and things without confusing them with the world of make believe. Even preschoolers may have trouble with stories about giants and witches. As their ability to use language grows, so will their understanding of the differences between real and pretend. For now, they are not ready for far-flung fantasy. That will come later.

Read It!

Goodnight Moon

(by Margaret Wise Brown/illus. by Clement Hurd, HarperCollins) Your child will soon know by heart the simple, soothing rhyme and rhythm of this classic bedtime book. Small children easily relate to the delaying tactics of the small bunny in his great green room who says goodnight to all the things in his sight, from a bowl full of mush and his comb and brush, to a quiet old lady who is whispering hush. This is available in a sturdy board book, but the size and colors in the traditional version are somewhat preferable. You may want to bring home both so your toddler can "read" the pictures independently. Spanish edition available. Also recommended, **Kiss Good Night** by Amy Hest/illus. by Anita Jeram.

Play It!

Goodnight Game   Language

Like the classic bunny in this well loved story, your toddler will enjoy saying goodnight to all the inanimate things in his room. Make this part of the bedtime ritual. It may take a little longer, but it's a comforting way to make the transition to sleep.

First Books for Older Toddlers

Sky Gazing

Make a point of looking in the night sky for the moon and the stars. Star gazers love being the first to spot a star. Remember this rhyme?

> Twinkle, twinkle, little star
> How I wonder what you are!
>> Up above the world, so high
>> Like a diamond in the sky.
> Twinkle, twinkle, little star
> How I wonder what you are!

Variation: Use the start of the new day for a silly Good Morning Game. Practice saying good morning to your child and the many playthings and familiar objects that are used each day.

You Win!

Make a lullaby or two part of your nightly ritual. Don't worry about singing on key. To your baby your voice is the one they'd choose over all others. Make the songs you sing more personal, insert your baby's name in the lyrics. Enjoy your American Idol status. (It won't last!)

WHAT THEY LEARN. Rituals around bedtime are not just a way to stall going to sleep. That last drink, the special song, the backrub, and final kisses good-night are predictable rituals that comfort a toddler as he releases himself to sleep.

Read It!

Does A Kangaroo Have a Mother, Too?

(by Eric Carle, HarperCollins) Does a kangaroo have a mother, too? Toddlers will like answering the repetitive questions about each of the animal pairs with a knowing "Yes! Just like you and me." A big concept book for beginners. Available in Spanish.

I Love My Mommy Because...

and **I Love My Daddy Because...**

(by Laurel Porter-Gaylord/illus. by Ashley Wolff, Dutton) These two little books take the same concept to the next level. Both celebrate the many ways that mommies and daddies care for their little ones. Charming illustrations include animal pairs and their loving ways. Both end with a child and parent. Proper names of animals and their young are provided, so this is a book that can be enjoyed for naming games, later. Available in Spanish.

Play It!

Make-A-Book   **Language**

Use photos to make a sturdy little family album that baby can enjoy independently. Photos with baby and family members are sure to be a hit. Use a small photo album, the kind they give away at the photo store (be sure there are no staples or spirals that can become choking hazards when baby tastes them). Use these photo storybooks to tell your baby stories about the person pictured.

Peek-a-Boo Song Game   Music

Your homemade family book can be used to play a little singing game. Sing these words to the melody of "Where is Thumbkin?"

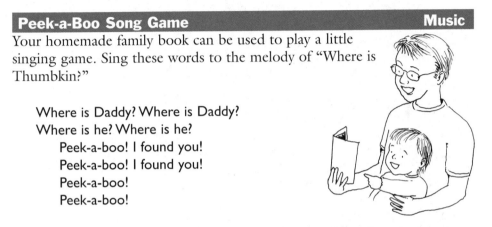

> Where is Daddy? Where is Daddy?
> Where is he? Where is he?
> > Peek-a-boo! I found you!
> > Peek-a-boo! I found you!
> > Peek-a-boo!
> > Peek-a-boo!

Repeat the song, changing the person you are searching for.

Where is Dad dy?   Where is Dad dy?   Where is he?   Where is he?   Peek a boo! I found you!

Peek   a   boo!   I   found   you!   Peek   a   boo!   Peek   a   boo!

WHAT THEY LEARN. Knowing and naming family members is fun, and playing peek-a-boo is a favorite — they can even play it with people who are not there!

Read It!

Big Red Barn

(by Margaret Wise Brown/illus. by Felicia Bond, Harper-Collins) With the same kind of soothing cadence as her classic *Goodnight Moon,* here M.W. Brown captures a day on the farm where the animals live, play, and go to sleep...

"By the big red barn,
In the great green field,
There was a pink pig
Who was learning to squeal..."

This not only works as a knowing and naming book with animal sounds, but also follows the events of a day and night when the animals settle down to sleep. Available in Spanish.

Play It!

Who Is Missing?   Visual memory

Put three toy animals in plain sight. Tell your child to look at the animals and then turn around (no peeking!) Say "I'm going to take one animal away. Can you figure out which one is missing?" When your child looks again, one of the creatures is missing. Can your child remember what he saw, to figure out which animal is missing?

WHAT THEY LEARN. Both book and song are fun ways for children to learn the names of farm animals and the sounds they make. In the Who Is Missing? game, children must use their memory as well as the ability to observe and recall.

Old MacDonald Game   Dramatic play

If your toddler has a miniature farm with animals, use them as you sing Old MacDonald. Toddlers like to chime in on the verse and, thanks to the repetition, they soon catch on. Move the animal you are singing about as you add each new verse.

Old MacDonald had a farm,
E I E I Oh!
And on this farm he had a sheep,
E I E I Oh!
With a baa baa here
and a baa baa there
Here a baa, There a baa,
Everywhere a baa baa
Old MacDonald had a farm,
E I E I Oh!

With older toddlers and preschoolers, make this into a cumulative song, repeating each of the animals and its sound as they are added. Having the animals in sight helps to remind the singers as they go through the line-up of animals.

Old Mac Do nald had a farm   E I E I Oh!   And on that farm he had a cow

E I E I Oh!   With a moo moo here and a moo moo there

Here a moo There a moo Ev ery where a moo moo Old Mac Do nald had a farm   E I E I Oh!

Read It!

Polar Bear, Polar Bear, What Do You Hear?

(by Bill Martin, Jr./illus. by Eric Carle, Henry Holt) Eric Carle's bold and brilliant beasts and Martin's simple but rhythmic rhyme make perfect harmony! Young listeners love chiming in on the repetitive, predictable telling. Also see *Brown Bear, Brown Bear, What Do You See?* Both available in Spanish.

Play It!

I Went to the Zoo   Concepts/Language/Dramatic Play

Borrow the refrain of "Polar Bear, Polar Bear . . ." as you pull your child's toy animals out one at a time. Before long your child will be adding animals as you both say…"I went to the zoo and what did I hear? A little lion growling at me!"

Make a "zoo" for the animals with a collection of shoe boxes or blocks that your child can continue to play with alone. This kind of game takes on even more interest after you really have gone to the zoo!

My Trip to the Zoo Book. Take some of those photographs from your visit to the zoo and put them in a small plastic photo album. Write names of animals on each page. Older toddlers can dictate a story about your visit together. Slip the text into the album. They will enjoy recounting their experience while at the same time revisiting the names of the animals.

We Went to the Zoo. Take turns adding to this story:

> We went to the zoo and we saw a <u>monkey</u>.
> We went to the zoo and we saw a <u>monkey</u> and a <u>lion</u>.
> We went to the zoo and we saw a <u>monkey</u> and a <u>lion</u> and an <u>elephant</u>.

As you play, try adding funny creatures that would not be in a zoo, such as a dragon or a unicorn.

WHAT THEY LEARN.
These are games that stretch language and memory.

Read It!

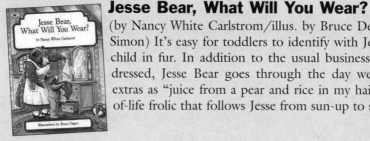

Jesse Bear, What Will You Wear?

(by Nancy White Carlstrom/illus. by Bruce Degen, Little Simon) It's easy for toddlers to identify with Jesse Bear, a child in fur. In addition to the usual business of getting dressed, Jesse Bear goes through the day wearing such extras as "juice from a pear and rice in my hair." A slice-of-life frolic that follows Jesse from sun-up to sun-down.

Play It!

Power Dressing   Developing Dexterity

Toddlers are better at taking clothes off than putting them on. Giving them easy-to-pull-on and -off clothes for their dolls or teddy bear gives them a chance to discover how clothes work. Dress up one of their big bears with baby-sized socks, shirt, and hat. Bigger is better and easier to get on and off.

Zippy Toddler Trick

Toddlers love to experiment with fasteners of all kinds. Zippers are fascinating but usually the zips (and buttons and laces) on learn-to-dress-dolls are more frustrating than useful. A cosmetic bag with a solid zipper will be a lot more interesting. Put crackers or a few favorite toys inside a zipped bag and let your toddler figure out how to get the bag open. This is a good one to keep your tot busy while you are preparing dinner. Just be sure the tag on the zipper is solidly attached. Add a piece of ribbon to the tag to make it easier to pull.

Power Choosing   Making Choices

Older toddlers often have strong opinions about what they want to wear. One way to avoid confrontations over totally inappropriate choices is to offer two choices, either of which will be fine for the occasion. So many things must be decided by grownups for young children, that giving them small but acceptable choices with simple things allows them a sense of power and independence. Choosing between a banana or an apple; or the red shirt or the blue will not make a difference to their well-being. In fact, doing so can diminish some of the friction that often comes as older tots struggle with their desire for greater independence.

WHAT THEY LEARN. Learning to handle clothes builds skills for independence.

Read It!

I Love Trucks

(by Philemon Sturges/illus. by Shari Halpern, HarperCollins) Little ones who are beginning to notice the many kinds of trucks in the world will love this colorful book with trucks that gobble trash, make concrete, dump, dig, sweep the streets, and so much more. Told in lilting verse, this is fun to hear and look at. Unlike the real things that roll away, these are available to pore over. Also perfect for truck lovers, Byron Barton's *Trucks*, and another favorite, *Truck Song* by Diane Siebert, for older toddlers.

Play It!

Make A Truck	Dramatic Play

A box that is big enough to climb in and out of will become a favorite "vehicle" of little pretenders. Put the child's name on the side of the truck and add headlights or other decorations. You can fuel your child's imagination by asking him where he's driving or telling her to please deliver your packages today. Young children don't really need all the realistic props to transform a box into a bus or a truck. Once they make the leap into pretend, the steering wheel and sound effects are in their mind's eye.

Make A Garage   Dramatic Play

Toy stores have mini-garages with ramps and elevators and all sorts of gimmicks. But you can also use a simple box to create a garage for parking small trucks and cars. Cut door flaps that lift. Older tots may like to paint their garage box; some will want you to add signs for gas and air and oil. Helping your child make such a building is a great way to foster the idea of using familiar things for pretend play.

Car & Truck Wash   Water Play

If you have a collection of ride-on vehicles at home or in your neighborhood, open a pretend car wash! Provide young workers with small pails of soap & water, sponges, and towels. This is a great group activity on a hot summer day to keep industrious pretenders busy for a long time.

WHAT THEY LEARN.
Along with role-playing, older toddlers are fascinated with any chores that involve making sudsy bubbles and puddles with soap and water. Seeing how the water changes the color of the cars and how air dries the water are all part of the fun of these early science investigations into the world of soap and water.

Read It!

Chugga Chugga Choo Choo

(by Kevin Lewis/illus. by Daniel Kirk, Hyperion) "Sun's up! Morning's here. Up and at 'em, / engineer..." These are the opening lines of an action-packed toy train story, told in full-steam-ahead rhyme and bold illustrations. Just the ticket for little engineers who love their toy trains. The repetitive refrain, "Chugga-chugga choo-choo, whistle blowing, Whoooooooo! Whoooooooooo!" is likely to be echoed when you read and they play. Younger train buffs will also enjoy Donald Crews' *Freight Train* (HarperCollins), but *Chugga Chugga Choo Choo* has delicious language that makes it a great read-aloud.

Play It!

Chugga! Chugga! Game   Transportation/dramatic play

Toy trains are a favorite of toddlers. Look for chunky trains that do not have small props or parts that can be a choking hazards. Add props that can be used for dramatic play:

• animals, cars, trucks, and people scaled to the size of trains
• blocks for buildings and bridges and roadways for cars and trucks
• a small shoe box with holes cut out makes a good tunnel

Without turning play into a quiz session, encourage your child to tell you about the mini-world he is creating. Chances are, he'll have lots to tell.

Enlarge upon his explanations by using position words that make such concepts more concrete and memorable. Even toy trains can go *into, through,*

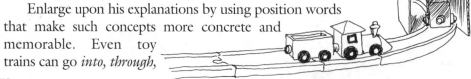

and *out of* tunnels; *over, under,* and *across* bridges; *around, behind, in front of,* and *next to* other trains. Learning these concepts through play is easier and far more meaningful than pages of a workbook.

Sing It!

This is a favorite song, easily learned since there is so much repetition. Encourage your child to follow your lead with words and motions.

She'll be com in' 'round the moun tain when she comes (Toot! Toot!) She'll be

com in' 'round the moun tain when she comes(Toot! Toot!) She'll be com in' 'round the moun tain, she'll be

com in' 'round the moun tain, she'll be com in' 'round the moun tain when she comes!(Toot! Toot!)

Other verses:

Oh, we'll all go out to meet her when she comes (Hi, Babe!)
[Wave your arm to greet Babe.]
She'll be driving six white horses when she comes (Whoa, there!)
[Pull the reins.]

You'll have to sleep with Grandma when she comes!
[Make a snoring sound twice.]

We'll all have chicken and dumplings when she comes (Yum! Yum!)
[Rub your tummy!]

WHAT THEY LEARN. Dramatic play develops children's ability to use their imagination and spin their own stories. These are important underpinnings for reading and writing stories.

Read It!

Over in the Meadow

(by Ezra Jack Keats, Viking) This is one of many versions of a classic counting rhyme that also introduces children to familiar animals and what they do. It's fun to count the animals on each double page spread or, next time you read it, have your little listeners act the actions and sounds out.

Play It!

Sing a Book   **Music and Math**

"Over In the Meadow" is an old song about animals that you and your child will enjoy playing. As you sing it, use gestures that reinforce the words. Use your fingers to show how many critters you are singing about — as in "little turtle one," "little fishies two," etc. Use your hands or arms to dig like a turtle, move your arm to swim like a fish, flap your wings as you *tu-whoo* like the owls. Making these kinds of motions gives meaning to the words.

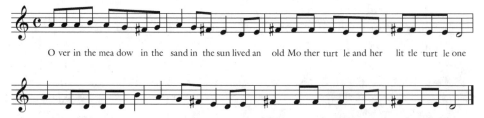

O ver in the mea dow in the sand in the sun lived an old Mo ther turt le and her   lit tle turt le one

Dig! said the Mo ther I   dig! said the one so they   dug and they dug   in the sand and the sun

Counting Games: One, Two, Three, Four

Older toddlers love to count — any excuse will do. It's fun to count as you:
- climb steps together
- give each person two crackers for their soup
- drop blocks into a container
- spot red cars on the road

Make spotting numbers an everyday part of life. How many numbers can you spot?
- on buses, buildings, trucks
- on clothes, packages, phones

WHAT THEY LEARN. Playing with numbers in multiple informal ways helps children get the notion of how useful numbers can be in the real world. The object is not to see how high they can count — numbers should have meaning. Better to count to five and understand what those numbers mean, than to turn numbers into meaningless gibberish. Counting is not then a trick that kids can do, but rather a useful skill.

Clap It Back Game. Tell your child you're going to play a counting game . . . but he shouldn't say the number — he should listen, and clap it back. Start with a simple two-beat clap. Can he clap that back? Try four claps. Can he clap that back? You can vary the beat and see if he can repeat the same number of claps with the same beat.

Read It!

Brown Bear, Brown Bear, What Do You See?

(by Bill Martin Jr. & Eric Carle, Henry Holt) Toddlers soon know the repetitive lines of this classic book and anticipate what animal comes next. This takes "knowing and naming" to a new level by introducing color words to the story. Your toddler will be learning the names of the animals as well as the colors the artist has used. In fact, the colors and textures of the animal collage are part of what makes this such a memorable book. Available in Spanish.

Play It!

Glue It!   Art

Artists sometimes tell stories with paint or drawings, but some do so with collages made by cutting and pasting materials into interesting images. Take inspiration from Eric Carle's glorious images and introduce your older toddler to the pleasures of messy sensory play involved in pasting. White glue in a dish is easier to use than the squeeze bottle — young artists are apt to squeeze the bottle dry. They'll learn more about the process if they use a brush or fingers to spread glue to surface and pat their collage materials down.

Keep a box of scrap fabric, paper, cardboard, old cards, and gift wraps that children can use for their own collages. The objective is to make a bumpy creation or one with many textures rather than a realistic picture of something.

Make a "Feeling" Collage

You'll need a collection of textured scrap materials which you'll probably find in your home, such as:

- bumpy cardboard from cookie packages
- smooth foil
- colored yarn
- ribbon
- sandpaper
- old greeting cards
- cellophane
- cotton balls
- fabric scraps
- bubble wrap
- tissue paper

You'll also need:

- glue
- cardboard & construction paper to mount objects

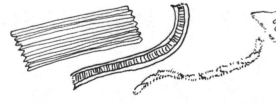

Talk about how various materials feel and how they can be used to make a picture that is bumpy or smooth or a mix of many textures. Once kids have had fun exploring, they may like making a "smooth" or "scratchy" collage. Most often children get caught up with the variety of the materials rather than making anything that's all of a kind.

WHAT THEY LEARN.
Along with the fine motor skills involved in cutting and pasting, children make design decisions as they arrange their "feeling" collages. They also enlarge their vocabulary for describing the textures of the materials they are using.

Read It!

Color Kittens

(by Margaret Wise Brown/illus. by Alice & Martin Provensen, Golden) These playful kittens have been mixing it up, introducing generations of children to colors and how they combine to make new colors. Probably the best follow-up fun for this book is to find a variety of ways for kids to mix some colors of their own.

Play It!

Blurry Blends   Art

Using food coloring or watercolors on absorbent paper produces very different effects. In fact, after whole sheets of paper are colored and dried, they can be used for making pretty gift-wraps or placemats. Simply making blends by folding the paper in different ways is a fascinating experience without regard to an end product.

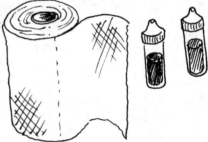

You'll need:

- paper towels
- food coloring or watery tempera paints

Do a few of these with your child and then step back. Kids will like doing this again and again:

• Demonstrate how to fold paper into triangles or smaller squares or wide accordion folds.

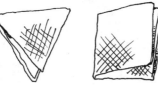 

• Dip corners into different colors of watery paint or squeeze food coloring onto the corners. Let the colors run into each other.
• Open the paper folds and see what interesting designs have formed.

Call child's attention to the mirror images that may have formed. Dry the paintings and save for other projects.

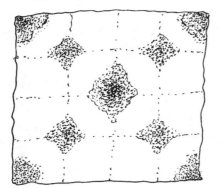

WHAT THEY LEARN.
These hands-on projects are a great way to learn more about the wonder of mixing colors.

Read It!

Carlo Likes Colors

(by Jessica Spanyol, Candlewick) Carlo, a giraffe, likes noticing the colors in his busy world. Unlike many other color-concept books, this one is clear and uncomplicated and the colors are not ambiguous. Multiple objects of one color, including black and white, are shown on each spread, and they are labeled for knowing and naming.

Play It!

Orange Day	Color concepts

Declare "Orange (or Green, Yellow, or Red) Day": On Orange Day, plan your meals around orange foods. Obviously you'll have oranges, American cheese, sweet potatoes, carrots — to name but a few. Of, course, blue day is tough unless blueberries are in season! You can also dress accordingly.

Splat & Splot Game	Art Exploration

You'll need:

- jars of red, yellow and blue washable tempera paint
- big pieces of paper
- paint brushes or eye dropper

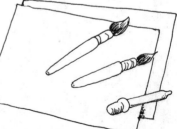

Remember how amazing it was when you discovered the magic of "splat" painting? Save plenty of scrap paper for this project. Once kids get started, they like do this simple trick again and again.

First Books for Older Toddlers

Step 1. Demonstrate how to drip a few splats and splots of paint in the middle of a sheet of paper.

Step 2. Fold the paper and show how you spread the paint by rubbing the fold. Open it up and WOW! What does it look like?
Variations: Start with a single color. Introduce a

WHAT THEY LEARN. Children are just beginning to explore the nature of paints — the colors; the way paint spreads on paper and the way it feels. Young painters don't purposefully make pictures that represent things. The blot on the page may look like something, but that is purely accidental. Talk about the color or the way it fills the page; don't worry about naming it. For now, just the act of painting is a pleasing experience.

second color that will blend to make a new color — a fun way to discover how red and yellow mix to make orange. Talk about the new color and the design. When it's dry, suggest adding "features" to their fantastic creations.

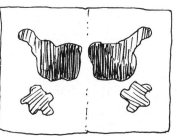

Read It!

Fish Eyes

(by Lois Ehlert, Harcourt) There isn't much text, but this little book reinforces color words as well as shapes and simple counting skills. As in *The Very Hungry Caterpillar*, the pages have cut-out holes that toddlers like to poke their finger into and note the color that is coming next. This also introduces the concept of one more, thanks to the little fish who appears in each spread.

Play It!

Color Detective Game   Color concepts

You can play this game anywhere — in a waiting room, a restaurant, or for stay-at-home fun. No special equipment needed — just use your eyes! To play: Make up riddles about things that are in clear view. Give a color clue plus others, for example: "I see something in this room that is red and round and crunchy to eat."

Post-It Color Game

Older toddlers like playing games as they learn color names. As children are learning color names, play the Post-It game: "Let's see how many things we can you find in this room that are green!" Put a Post-It on everything you see that is green.

WHAT THEY LEARN. Children don't need workbooks to learn colors. These are concepts best learned in the context of everyday experiences. Talk about the color of things they are playing with, wearing, or eating.

Clean-Up Color Sorting Game   Color Concepts

Picking up cars and trucks or plastic building blocks is more fun for toddlers when you do it by color. "Let's put all the red ones in the basket first." Then move on with, "Let's see who can find all the yellow ones." Use baskets or containers for like objects — for example, keep all their cars in one basket, toy figures or animals in another, blocks in another. Such games develop language, classifying, and sorting skills while reinforcing concepts such as color or size.

Mary Wore a Red Dress

You can change the names, colors and clothes in this old folk song and turn dressing into a game.

> Matthew wears his yellow shirt, yellow shirt, yellow shirt;
> Matthew wears his yellow shirt all day long.

> Matthew wears his white socks, his white socks, his white socks;
> Matthew wears his white socks all day long.

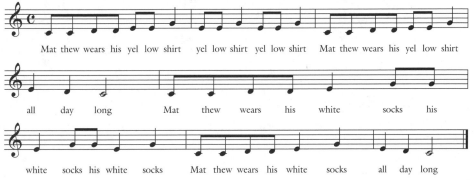

Mat thew wears his yel low shirt   yel low shirt yel low shirt   Mat thew wears his yel low shirt

all   day   long   Mat   thew   wears   his   white   socks   his

white   socks his white   socks   Mat thew wears his white   socks   all   day   long

Read It!

If You're Happy and You Know It!

(by Jane Cabrera, Holiday House) Cabrera gives this old song new life with creatures stamping their feet, clapping their hands, and flapping their arms. A playful way to combine animal names, body parts, and action.

Sing It!

Sing a Song   **Music & self image**

If you're happy and you know it, clap your hands [clap, clap]
If you're happy and you know it, clap your hands [clap, clap]
If you're happy and you know it, then you really ought to show it
If you're happy and you know it, clap your hands [clap, clap]

Change the action with each verse . . .

. . .stamp your feet	. . .show your tongue
. . .wiggle your nose	. . .click your teeth
. . .blink your eyes	. . .hop on one leg
. . .touch your toes	. . .hold your elbows
. . .hold your ears	

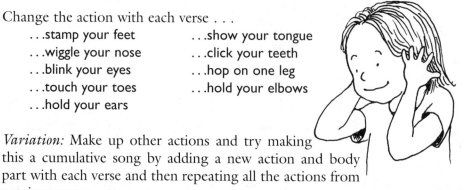

Variation: Make up other actions and try making this a cumulative song by adding a new action and body part with each verse and then repeating all the actions from previous verses.

If you're hap py and you know it clap your hands (clap clap) If you're

hap py and you know it clap your hands (clap clap) If you're hap py and you know it Then you

real ly ought to show it If you're hap py and you know it clap your hands (clap clap)

Play It!

What's Missing?

Older toddlers cannot draw a human figure, but they will be amused to tell you what is missing from your drawing. Start with a face first and draw just a nose. Ask your child, "Oh, oh! What's missing?" Continue drawing until you have a complete face or body. You can sing a little rendition of "Head and Shoulders Knees and Toes" and have your child touch those parts as you sing together.

WHAT THEY LEARN. Names of body parts are easier to learn through active play. Here you have games that reinforce language as well as sharpening visual skills. Make the drawings simple or detailed to match your child's knowledge and even stretch it a bit.

Read It!

Eric Hill

Where's Spot?

(by Eric Hill, Putnam) Spot is the pup who made lift-the-flap books popular. You may have had them when you were little. Like all books in a series, some are better than others. In this original story, Spot the pup is missing! Where can he be? Lift the flaps and see! Be prepared: Little hands may not be able to lift without a rip. 2 & up.

Little Mysteries

Lift-the-flap books are favorites of toddlers. What makes them so appealing? They have an element of surprise and peek-a-boo playfulness. You'll find Spot, Maisy, Clifford, and others in similar formats. There are dozens of choices, but some are flimsy and easily ripped; many make little or no sense story-wise; others have die-cut flaps that are sharp. You'll need to try before you buy.

Where is Baby's Mommy?

(by Karen Katz, Simon & Schuster) Where is Mommy? Behind the chair? Under the table? This lift-the-flap book is a playful game that tots will no doubt enjoy playing. A perfect choice to share for lap time. A little suspense plus a lot of position concepts.

Play It!

Where's Teddy?   Active play

After sharing this toddler-sized mystery, play a little mystery game of your own. Tell your toddler that you have hidden one of his plush teddy bears. Ask him, "Is Teddy behind the chair? Is Teddy under the bed? Is Teddy in the closet? Where can Teddy be?" Of

WHAT THEY LEARN. Following your clues requires careful listening and expands their understanding of position words such as *under* or *behind*. This is a game they'll enjoy playing more than once — just change the clues and locations.

course one of your clues is going to lead your tot to the bear for a happy reunion!

Open Shut Them!   Language Concepts

Just like opening and shutting the flaps, here is a favorite fingerplay song to play.

Open *[Open fingers]*
Shut them *[Make a fist]*
Open *[Repeat . . .]*
Shut them
Give a little clap
[Clap hands together]
Open, shut them
Open, shut them
Put them in your lap *[put hands in lap]*

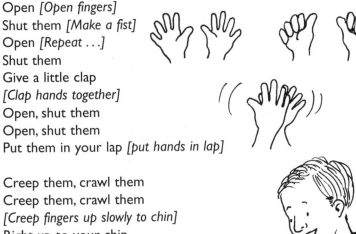

Creep them, crawl them
Creep them, crawl them
[Creep fingers up slowly to chin]
Right up to your chin
Creep them, crawl them
Creep them, crawl them
[Creep fingers up slowly to chin]
BUT do not let them in!

Read It!

Where Does Maisy Live?

(by Lucy Cousins, Candlewick) Where does everybody's favorite mouse live? Does she live in a pigpen? Lift the flap! "Oink, oink, the pigs live here!" Does she live in the stable? Lift the flap. "Neigh! The horses live here." Toddlers love the predictable repetitive guessing game, the humor, and feeling totally wise as they shout "No!" even before they lift the flap. Sturdy construction allows for repeated readings and solo looking. Available in Spanish.

Play It!

Where Do You Live?   Problem solving

Talk about where you and your toddler live. Who else lives with your family? Does Daddy live here? Does a big brother or sister live here? Does Grandma live here? How about a doggy or a kitten? As you talk about those who live in your house, throw in a few folks who absolutely do not live there. Does Big Bird live here? How about Barney? Tots will see the humor of this and enjoy shouting, "No!" to your ridiculous questions!

Does Big Bird live here?

No!

You're Hot! You're Cold!   Problem solving

This is like the game "Where's Teddy?" but harder! Instead of naming places to look, in this game your toddler will be listening to hot and cold clues and have to remember what the clues mean. Tell your tot to go in the next room (no peeking!), and say you are going to hide Teddy or Elmo somewhere in the room. When your tot comes back, give some hints. Explain that when he gets near the toy you'll tell him, "You're getting hot"; when he's going the wrong way you'll say, "You're cold!" Start the game. When he is far from Elmo, tell him, "You're cold . . .very cold." For beginners, you may want to leave an arm or leg peeking out so success is assured.

Make a Book   Language Concepts

Use a small photo album with photos of your home in it. You can even label the book "My Home" with your child's name on the cover. Put photos of the outside and inside of your home in the book. Talk about the names of the rooms, the colors in the house, and who lives there. Children love having homemade books that they can "read" independently as well as with you. This is one of those open-ended opportunities where the story can change every time!

WHAT THEY LEARN. These activities help children know and name the rooms in their house and the members of their families — it's "knowing and naming" at a higher level.

Read It!

Five Little Monkeys Jumping on the Bed

(illus. by Eileen Christelow, Clarion) This classic rhyme is good fun to act out as a finger play or with toy animals. Children especially love the falling down part and shaking their fingers to warn the naughty monkeys! Counting backwards is built in, so it's a funny introduction to subtraction. But this is more about repetition and playfulness than math. Also, the classic song, **Five Little Ducks** (illus. by Pamela Paparone, North-South) builds on the same concepts.

Play It!

Five Little Monkeys Fingerplay   **Waiting Room Game**

Toddlers like watching and trying to do finger plays with you. This is a fun one because it has both naughty and bossy parts.

Five little monkeys jumping on the bed —
[wiggle the fingers of one hand behind your other arm]

One fell off and bumped his head
[put your hand on your head].

Mother called the doctor
[pretend to hold a phone to your ear]
and the doctor said,

"No more monkeys jumping on the bed!"
[shake your finger]

Five Little Teddy Bears — Dramatic play

Put five teddy bears or rabbits on the edge of the bed. Help your tot make them jump as you say the rhyme out loud. One little bear will fall off each time and both of you can act out the phone call to the doctor and the warning by shaking your finger and saying, "No more teddy bears jumping on the bed!"

Bake a Number

Baking involves numbers in many ways, but keep it playful. Toddlers will like putting ingredients in while you do the counting. Use a biscuit recipe or use a mix. Roll the dough into rounds and count out loud as you put them on the baking pan.

Young bakers will also have fun baking their numbers. Roll the dough into snake shapes and twist the snakes into numerals. Bake number biscuits for each person's age.

WHAT THEY LEARN. Counting the cutout shapes gives children a concrete way to see what we mean when we talk about one, two, three.

Read It!

The Going to Bed Book

(by Sandra Boynton, Little Simon) Here's a jaunty rhyme that will put the bounce in bedtime. Likely to become a chant that your child will be chiming in on as you read or even get ready for bed. Available in Spanish.

Play It!

Row, Row, Row Your Boat   Music / Tub Fun

Bedtime and bathtime go hand in hand. It's a perfect time for your undivided attention. Forget about the phone, work, whatever—make bathtime a relaxing playtime that sets the stage for bedtime.

Here's a funny variation of "Row, Row, Your Boat." Put one or more of your toddler's toy boats in the tub and line up some of his plastic toy animals and people. Sing, "Row, row, row your horse, gently down the stream. Bubbly, bubbly, bubbly, bubbly, life is but a dream!" Continue as you both keep adding passengers until — oh, oh — over they go! Time to sing and load them up again!

WHAT THEY LEARN.

A fun way to learn the names of the animals and do a little water play investigation.

Sing Them Clean!

Use the melody of "Row, Row, Row Your Boat" to get through other clean-up routines. Adding a little song may make these moments less of a struggle and more of a game.

Brush, brush, brush your teeth,
brush your teeth today.
Mary, Mary *[use your child's name]*
brush your teeth.
Brush! Yes, that's the way!

Scrub, scrub, scrub your knees,
Scrub your knees today.
Johnny, Johnny scrub your knees.
Scrub the dirt away!

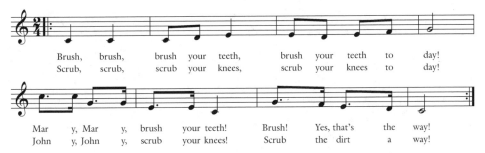

| Brush, | brush, | brush | your | teeth, | brush | your | teeth | to | day! |
| Scrub, | scrub, | scrub | your | knees, | scrub | your | knees | to | day! |

| Mar | y, Mar | y, | brush | your teeth! | Brush! | Yes, that's | the | way! |
| John | y, John | y, | scrub | your knees! | Scrub | the dirt | a | way! |

Read It!

Hands
Are Not for
Hitting

Hands Are Not For Hitting

(by Martha Agassi/illus. by Marieka Heinlen, Free Spirit) Here's a book that makes no bones about the big idea that hands are not for hitting others. It's a concept book that talks about the many positive things we can do with hands — a big concept that toddlers and preschoolers need to get hold of, though the message may take time to deliver.

Play It!

Play Dough	Art/ Feeling / Concepts

Playing with pre-made or homemade dough is marvelous for twos who love pounding, poking, rolling, crumbling, and hands-on exploring. This is an acceptable way to use little hands — even for hitting! At this stage the finished product is unimportant. The focus is on smashing a lump flat, or pulling it apart into small pieces, or mixing blue and yellow to get green. Many toy sets come with tools and cutters, but for beginners getting their hands into the dough and exploring the material is what it's all about.

If you buy pre-made dough, you may need to handle it to get it soft and pliable enough for little hands. Dough should be used with supervision in an established place for messy play. Beginners will try to taste: It's non-toxic but not for eating.

Making Dough Game

Save money by making your own dough with this homemade play-dough recipe. Kids enjoy getting their hands into the bowl and helping to mix up dough, which can be stored in a covered container. Mix together:

- 1 cup of flour,
- half a cup of salt,
- a few drops of vegetable oil,
- enough water to form a dough.

Add the water slowly, as it may become too sticky if you add too ~~much~~ and too dry if you don't have enough.

Multi-colored Dough: Dough can be colored with a splash of tempera paint or food coloring. After the white dough is ready, break it apart in three balls. Knead red paint into one, yellow into another, and blue into a third. Store dough in plastic baggies.

Demonstrate: Take a bit of blue dough and yellow dough and knead it together. What happens? Talk about how the colors of the dough mix, just like the liquid paints, to make new colors. Encourage your child to talk about how the dough feels and what happens when she rolls it, pricks it, pounds it. Eventually, you may want to add plastic forks, knives, and a round block for a rolling pin. But give your toddler lots of time to do this with her hands.

WHAT THEY LEARN. Develop hand and finger power as well as investigating the way powdery substances can change when we add liquids. Use colorful sensory language as you mix the dough together. Add colors and talk about how two colors blend to make a new color.

Read It!

Here Are My Hands

(by Bill Martin Jr. & John Archambault/illus. by Ted Rand, Holt) This is more than a book about hands. With utter simplicity, the rhymes in this sturdy board book name parts of the body and what they do. A charming book that features a multicultural cast of children from all over the world.

Play It!

Creative Exploration	Self Image/Art/Concepts

Older toddlers love making swirls as well as fingertip and whole hand/whole footprint designs with finger paint. Keeping the art is not nearly as important as getting into the paint! If you feel the need to capture the moment, use individual sheets of paper, or use a long sheet of shiny shelving paper, which can be used for gift-wrap. Cover the area and plan tub time next on your agenda!

Whole Hand Art	Creative Exploration

Long before older toddlers can handle a paintbrush with skill, they are well endowed for whole-hand and finger painting. In fact, even if you give young kids brushes, they are likely to get more on their hands than on the brush. Why? Kids are sensory learners, and feeling the texture and flow of the paint in their hands fits their learning style.

You'll need:
- fingerpaint: storebought or homemade*
- slick shelf paper
- a big washable tabletop or tray to work on

- a tub of water to wet down the paper
- plastic forks or comb
- smock or old shirt to cover clothes

*Recipe for Homemade Fingerpaint

Mix a cup of flour, a cup of water, and two tablespoons of liquid dishwashing detergent to an easy-to-spread, paste-like mixture. Adjust water if necessary.

Put some of the paste into several bowls or baggies and add a spoon of tempera paint or food coloring to each bowl or baggie.

Activity ideas

- Demonstrate how to make interesting designs with the fingertips or swirling shapes with whole hands.
- Add a second color to see how they combine to make a third color!
- Put a sheet of paper on the tray to lift a "print" of a design. But remember that young kids are not so concerned with making end products. It's the excitement of the moment and seeing how their actions cause reactions that they enjoy most.
- Talk about the shapes they are making: zigzags, swirls, and straight lines.

Keeping the Mess to a Minimum

Obviously this is a messy activity — maybe that's what makes it so appealing to kids. You can contain the mess somewhat by:

- using a large cookie sheet with a lip around it;
- dressing your tot in totally washable clothes;
- spreading a large plastic tablecloth or plastic bag over the work surface.

WHAT THEY LEARN. Unlike painting with a brush, finger painting puts them in direct contact with the material and the pure joy of mucking about.

Read It!

My Car

(by Byron Barton, Greenwillow) Bold images and simple text tell a small story about Sam, a man who loves his car. The story transports us through day and night, sun and rain. Clever Sam takes good care and obeys all the rules. Lucky Sam — when he gets to work he switches from driving a car to driving a big bus! For transportation lovers, this will get lots of mileage!

Play It!

Stop-&-Go Game   Active game

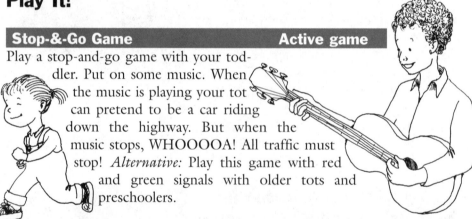

Play a stop-and-go game with your toddler. Put on some music. When the music is playing your tot can pretend to be a car riding down the highway. But when the music stops, WHOOOOA! All traffic must stop! *Alternative:* Play this game with red and green signals with older tots and preschoolers.

WHAT THEY LEARN. Learning to pay attention to and obey signals they hear or see is not as easy as it may seem. For young children, remembering what the signals mean is only the first part; a second, separate effort is actually doing it. Still, this is a fun way to develop their ability to integrate that information into action or inaction.

Playful Ways to Spin their Wheels

Once children have language, the ability to play at pretend blossoms. To encourage that kind of play, add some simple props. The younger the child, the more realistic, or literal, toys need to be.

Build a Ramp Game. Build a ramp for rolling cars and trucks up and down a hill of pillows. Race two cars and see which one goes downhill fastest. Use the words *up* and *down* to reinforce those concepts.

Make a Roadway Game. Make a roadway with a long line of blocks or masking tape and show your toddler how to run her vehicles over the road. Make simple tunnels with boxes or blocks that cars can go under.

Take a Drive. Demo how to drive little vehicles under tables, around chair legs, around a corner, behind a pillow. Add a little drama — stopping for gas, red lights, traffic jams. These are concrete ways to develop language concepts while modeling pretend play.

Read It!

Barnyard Dance

(by Sandra Boynton, Workman) Toddlers like to chime in to this rhythmic romp. Before you know it, older toddlers will know parts of this lively book by heart. Read it fast, read it slow, read it loud, or whisper it. It's more like a nonsense verse than a story, but that's the point. Playing with sounds and moving to rhythms give children playful connections to books and language.

Play It!

Music and Motion   **Music and Active Play**

Play various kinds of music to inspire children to move in different ways. Mix it up so that the pace and beat are distinctly different. Play your guitar, piano, drum, or use a mix of music from your CD collection. As they move to the music, encourage children to listen and follow the music. Toddlers will enjoy a silk scarf that flies on the breeze as they move about.

Music Makers. Toddlers can keep the beat and enjoy making music to go along with their dancing. Keep the raw material safe and easy to handle.

- Fill a plastic container or potato chip tube with a scoop full of Cheerios that will make a good rattle sound when shaken. Tape shut unless you don't mind if they spill.
- Give toddler a spoon and pot or a disposable pie tin with a short loop of ribbon to hold it. This allows it to vibrate when struck like a drum.

• Put a large piece of bubble wrap on the floor, put on some music, and let the fun begin as kids jump on the wrap and pop the bubbles. Use this with supervision since toddlers may want to taste the popping wrap.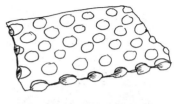

Hit It!

Toddlers and preschoolers love the power of this silly game. As they hit a pot or clang their cymbals you move to the beat with jerky movements. When the sound stops, you stop instantly. When they start again, you begin to move again. Toddlers will giggle themselves silly as they enjoy controlling your movements. Older kids will like reversing roles and moving to your beat.

WHAT THEY LEARN. Motion is what toddlers love best. Moving to music gives them a great way to develop balance and coordination and those big muscles.

Read It!

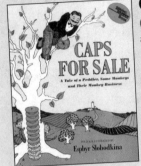

Caps for Sale

(by Esphyr Slobodkina, HarperCollins) Older toddlers and preschoolers see the humor of this "monkey see, monkey do" book. It's a little story of a peddler who takes a nap and wakes up to find that a tree full of monkeys have taken his caps. In fact, children love knowing where the caps are before the peddler discovers them. They also love chiming in on the repetitive "Give me back my caps!" and the monkeys' answer, "Tsz, tsz, tsz." Available in Spanish.

Play It!

This Is What I Like to Do   **Music/active play**

This is what I like to do
Wouldn't you like to do it too?
This is what I like to do
Now we'll all follow y-o-u!

Each singer/player acts out a motion, such as scratching head, hitting chest, wiggling fingers, funny face, spinning whole being. Others must follow

what the leader is doing and then come up with an original motion when it is their turn. A fun turn-taking game for parent and child.

Dress-up Clothes Collection

Older toddlers love dressing in grownups' clothes. Old hats, shoes, gloves, vests, and skirts are fine. So are pocketbooks, briefcases, jewelry, and scarves. Real things that parents have used often have more appeal than scaled-down costumes. Put them in a basket where kids can easily use them and put them away. Avoid items with buttons, beads and other small parts can be a choking hazard for kids who still mouth things.

WHAT THEY LEARN. Pretend play props for young children often needs to be more realistic than those needed for older children with greater imagination. Older children can turn a scarf into a bride's veil, a gown, or a cape. Twos and threes are still sorting out the names of things and how they are used. Imaginative flights of fancy will come later. Using your things gives them a sense of grown-up power that is not possible in the real world, but totally possible through pretend.

Read It!

Who Hops?

(by Katie Davis, Harcourt) Try this amusing concept book. Older toddlers will enjoy shouting "No!" when you ask, "Do cows hop?" This kind of upside-down humor is broad enough for a toddler's funny bone. This silly little book shows animals that do crawl, swim, fly, and hop, as well as those who do not. Davis sums it all up with a question about who can do all of these things and the child listener is on center stage! Available in Spanish.

Play It!

Act it Out   **Dramatic play**

After sharing this book it's fun to act it out. As you read the verse encourage tots to go through the motions and add their own. Add music to the action. Saint-Saëns' "Carnival of the Animals" is a perfect choice.

Woof!

Animal Riddles — Problem-solving

Using a mini-setting with animal figures, such as a zoo or a farm, put the animals in various locations upstairs, down, behind, in front of, next to, etc. Now give clues about one of the animals. Say, "I'm thinking of an animal that gives us milk, says moo, and is in front of the barn." or "I'm thinking of an animal that stands on two feet and is upstairs in the barn."

Who Moved? — Memory game

Line up three or four toy animals and tell your toddler to look at them, and then turn around. No peeking allowed! Now you remove one of the animals. Say, "OK, now you can look at the animals. Who is gone? Can you figure it out?"

WHAT THEY LEARN. These are games that build language and memory, and introduce science concepts that help children see differences and likenesses.

Read It!

Hug

(by Jez Alborough, Candlewick) A little chimp travels through the jungle in search of a hug. While he finds many other animals hugging, it's not until he finds his mommy that the little chimp is content. Told with few words and charming illustrations, this story is sure to lead to some hug time of your own. 2 & up.

When Mama Comes Home Tonight

(by Eileen Spinelli/illus. by Jane Dyer, Little Simon) Anticipating the end of day when Mama comes home from work, this is a sweet story that mirrors the lives of many families. Told in verse with watercolor illustrations, it sets the scene for the cozy reunion that makes the end of day so sweet. Available in Spanish.

Play It!

Hide & Seek Games   **Active games/family connections**

Where in the World is . . .?

Toddlers see the humor of your searching for something in plain sight that they can see. For example, pretend to search for a spoon, asking, "Did I put it in my pocket? Is it under the pillow? In your hat?" Tots love being so smart they can show you. Funnier yet, pretend to look for your toddler, and when he "finds" you, give him a big bear hug!

Oh, Where, Oh, Where Did My Baby Go?

Toddlers love playing hide-and-seek games with their whole beings now that they can toddle, walk, and eventually run out of sight. They may simply turn so they can't see you and laugh when they look at you or they may hide around a corner and giggle when they pop out to answer your call . . . "Where did my baby go?" End each round of hide and seek with a good hug and a happy "I found you!"

You found it!

See & Tell

Look at a book with pictures of several objects on a page. Ask your toddler if he can find something you wear on your feet or head or hands in the pictures. When he finds it, say, "You found it!"

Touch & Tell

Put three toys with distinctive textures in a bag. Ask your toddler to reach in and find the bumpy (round, hard, fluffy, etc.) toy without looking. When he pulls out the bumpy toy, say, "Peek-a-boo! You found it!"

WHAT THEY LEARN. These little hide-and-seek games are good fun and reinforce the bigger idea that out of sight is not out of mind. It's also a way of playing around with and feeling in control of mini-separations . . . people go away and they come back.

87

Read It!

Runaway Bunny

(by Margaret Wise Brown/illus by Clement Hurd, HarperCollins) "'If you run away,' said his mother, 'I will run after you. For you are my little bunny.'" In this delicious pretend game of "runaway," Mama Rabbit is never far behind. Toddlers can have the vicarious thrill of running away (as they often try to do — while looking over their shoulder to be sure you are there). A reassuring story that says Mama will be there for her little bunny — no matter what! Spanish edition available.

Play It!

Pawpaw Patch   **Active games/family connections**

A fun song to act out with motions. Encourage your child to lead the motions and you follow . . . like Mama Rabbit.

Pawpaw Patch

"Where, oh, where is dear little_____ [child's name]?
Where, oh, where is dear little_____?
Where, oh, where is dear little_____?
Way down yonder in the pawpaw patch.
[point over your shoulder to pawpaw patch]

Picking up pawpaws
[motion as if picking up something from ground]
Put them in your pocket
[pretend to put them in your pocket]

Picking up pawpaws, put them in your pocket—
Way down yonder in the pawpaw patch!

Change the name for each of the children and grown-ups who are singing.

Where oh where is dear lit tle (child's name) Where oh where is

dear lit tle (child's name) Where oh where is dear lit tle (child's name) way down yon der in the

paw paw patch Pick ing up paw paws put them in your pock et Pick ing up paw paws

put them in your pock et Pick ing up paw paws put them in your pock et

way down yon der in the paw paw patch!

Can You Do What I Do? Toddler Game

Use a full-length mirror to play a "Can you do what I do?" game. Use big and little motions from faces to toes. Getting kids to copy what you are doing is more than fun. It helps kids begin to focus on details and translate what they see into actions. Demonstrate a sequence of two motions — pat your head and then your tummy. Can he remember two motions? How about three?

WHAT THEY LEARN.

These interactive games between child and adult involve thinking up actions and also imitating actions of others through observation.

Read It!

Cows in the Kitchen

(by June Crebbin/illus. by Katherine McEwen, Candlewick) You are going to sing this book and before long, your toddler will be singing with you! Using the rhythm of "Skip to My Lou," this bouncy nonsense song is illustrated with cows prancing in the kitchen, pigs munching in the pantry, and sheep bouncing on the sofa while Tom Farmer sleeps. Great good fun with tons of repetitive rhymes and lines.

Play It!

Toddlers in the Kitchen   Props for Play

Keeping little ones busy while you are making a meal in the kitchen calls for some planning ahead. You don't want them underfoot in the hot areas where you are cooking. Still, they often need and want to be with you. Make a cupboard they can open and close available and stock it with safe-to-play-with items that you change from time to time.

Little Drummer   Eye Hand Coordination

Pots and pans are classic props for music making. Add a spoon, and they are ready for Drumming 101. Clang the lids and you have cymbals. Hold the pot lid and strike with a spoon and you have a different sound. Start with one pot and lid. Put some chunky plastic blocks in the pot for baby to fill and dump. Add another pot of a different size and let baby discover which lid fits on which pot — a bit of hands-on problem solving that will keep your baby occupied. For a quieter drum, try a plastic bowl with a strong plastic spoon.

Nesting Bowls   Nesting and Stacking 101

Most store-bought nesting toys involve fitting cups in size order. Often the pieces of such toys are lost before tots can do them. You will find that a stack of paper bowls or plates to nest works well, without any need for size order to gum up the works! Toddlers will enjoy taking the stack apart and, with a little encouragement and time, they'll work at nesting them back together. Try a clutch of paper cups, too. Cups are a bit more challenging to nest inside each other, but you can play a game of stacking them in a tower that tots will love knocking over.

Size Order   Advanced Nesting and Stacking

For more experienced hands, add a set of nested measuring cups of different sizes. WARNING: Steer clear of those with a ring that holds them together. That ring can be a choking hazard if it comes off. Provide other stacking and nesting items for older tots to take apart and put together. A set of mixing bowls, a set of plastic storage containers, or a set of cardboard boxes that fit into each other are all interesting materials to explore.

Read It!

I Went Walking

(by Sue Williams/illus. by Julie Vivas, Harcourt) One little child goes walking and meets an ever-growing menagerie of familiar animals. The crowd grows as the walk moves along. Color words are introduced, but this is not so much a know-your-colors book as it is an imaginative journey with lots of action to talk about along the way. Available in Spanish.

Play It!

Go Walking Game · Active Looking

On a walk it's fun to see how many animals you can spot along the way. When you come home you can talk about how, "I went for a walk and what did I see? I saw a pigeon, a brown dog, and a grey cat, looking at me!" Giving them things to look for and then to talk about adds to the shared moments of the day and expands their language and memory. On a future walk you might listen for animal sounds or look for stores with things to eat.

Follow the Leader

Oddly enough, toddlers can't really skip. It takes time to develop the coordination to do so, but they do love a good game of follow the leader. Any day that needs some giggles is ripe for romping through the house and changing gears by jumping, hopping, slithering, baby-stepping, or twirling. For starters, you can be the leader — but take turns! Toddlers have some great moves to show you!

Following the Leader

We're following the leader, the leader, the leader
We're following the leader, wherever he [she] may go!
We won't be home 'til morning, 'til morning, 'til morning
We won't be home 'til morning, wherever he [she] may go!

Variation: Use your toddler's animal collection to make a follow-the-leader game. If her teddy bear hops, then the rabbit must hop. If the rabbit is the leader and it wiggles across the floor, the teddy bear must do the same.

WHAT THEY LEARN. This game helps toddlers use their big motor skills, using their whole being as they observe and translate what they see to active big motor motions.

Read It!

The Very Hungry Caterpillar

(by Eric Carle, Philomel) This is one of those rare books that children enjoy from babyhood to early school. Baby will delight in poking a little finger into the holes as the little caterpillar feasts its way through the books. Preschoolers will enjoy the small story, the colorful illustrations, and the seemingly magic transformation to butterfly! Along with basic concepts of color and counting, this is a perfect little science book. Be sure to share it when butterflies can be spotted outdoors. Spanish edition available.

Play It!

What's Under that Rock?   Science/art

When you take your toddler for a walk, it's sometimes hard to slow down and allow them time to investigate the shape of a leaf, the birds on the lawn, a bug on a plant, a shell or rock on the beach. Yet taking the time to do so gives them a chance to observe first hand how a bug moves, a bird flies, and a rock feels.

Along with getting to feel at home in the world, these are opportunities for enlarging their vocabulary by "naming and knowing" and give meaning to concepts that are best learned through first-hand experiences. You may need to slow the pace of your walk, but stopping to look at what is under a rock, swimming in a puddle, or creeping on a leaf is the best way to introduce children to the beauties and mysteries of the natural world.

Tasting Party

Your toddler may be inspired by the very hungry caterpillar to try some fresh fruit. Have a tasting party one day. You can also have a mystery party on another day. Have your child close her eyes and taste a piece of fruit you put in her mouth. Can she tell from the texture, scent, taste what that fruit is? This is naming and knowing to the next level!

Abra-ca-dabra Art

Put a large piece of paper on a table. With your child, make squiggles and lines with a wax candle or a white crayon. It will appear that nothing is there. Now give your child a big paint brush and some watered-down tempera paint. What happens when she covers the paper with the paint? Abra-ca-dabra!

WHAT THEY LEARN. Toddlers are by nature curious. Keeping that curiosity alive and well means giving them ways of exploring the world. It's from these hands-on explorations that children learn best.

95

Read It!

Little Red Hen

The Little Red Hen
Byron Barton

(by Byron Barton, HarperFestival) This is a simple telling of the classic tale with the Little Red Hen asking for help as she plants the seeds, harvests and threshes the wheat, and makes the bread. In this telling, her little chicks help (as all little chicks should), but her friends Pig, Duck, and Cat refuse. In the end, Hen and her chicks get their reward while the others watch. There's a lot of "justice" served up in this little tale, but young listeners enjoy the vicarious thrill of refusing to help and then seeing the punishment fit the crime. Spanish edition available.

Play It!

Bake a Bread   **Kitchen Science**

If you have your own recipe, this is the time to stir it up and have your older toddler help. Make a mini loaf that can be enjoyed for a tea party. Even if you don't bake bread from scratch, you can easily bake biscuits or rolls from a pre-packaged mix. Talk about how the dough looks and feels when it goes in the oven. How does it look and feel when it comes out? Spread the bread or rolls with butter and enjoy as you share the retelling of the story.

First Books for Older Toddlers

This repetitive tale is fun to retell together. You don't have to use the words exactly as they are written. In fact, simply by "reading" the illustrations, it's possible to retell the story in your own words. Encourage your older toddler to chime in with some of the predictable repeated parts of the story. Over time your older toddler will be able to "read" more and more of the story to you and even to his teddy bear.

WHAT THEY LEARN. Children learn several important skills as they help retell a story with you. They are learning the mechanics of how a book works, from left to right and from front to back. They are also recalling the story, the sequence of the story, and interpreting the pictures to help them with the task. These are all key to becoming a reader.

Read It!

Splash!

(by Flora McDonnell, Candlewick) Two elephants in a sun drenched scene are "Hot, hot, hot!" In fact all the creatures in this charming little book are hot and finally cool off when they follow baby and mama elephant to the watering hole. What a relief as they splish, splash, and squirt the water!

Play It!

Splish! Splash! Look What's In My Bath!   **Science concepts**

Even in the dead of winter it's possible for babies and toddlers to enjoy the fun of water play! Tub time is ideal for watery experiments. Aside from the usual boats and rubber ducky, a lot of familiar household items make interesting tub toys.

- plastic colander
- plastic turkey baster
- plastic jars and cups for filling and spilling
- paper cups and paper bowls with and without holes

Going Down!

In the tub, use a variety of plastic containers (sandwich boxes, bowls, cups, and measuring cups) as "boats." Using a paper cup to fill up a boat, count

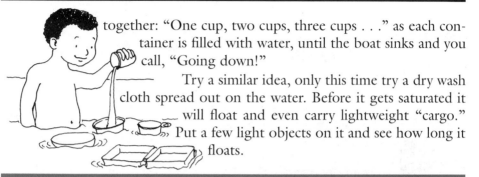

together: "One cup, two cups, three cups . . ." as each container is filled with water, until the boat sinks and you call, "Going down!"

Try a similar idea, only this time try a dry wash cloth spread out on the water. Before it gets saturated it will float and even carry lightweight "cargo." Put a few light objects on it and see how long it floats.

Count Down — Suds be Gone! Game

Rinsing suds out of hair is sometimes worrisome to kids. Let kids know how long they will have to count before all the soap is out. Try counting one hippopotamus, two rhinoceros . . . in order to slow down the count, or have your child guess how many cups of water it will take to get the job done. With kids who are fretful about shampooing, you may want to do their hair in the sink, instead of making bath time a hassle.

Hot! Hot! Hot!

To cool off on a really hot day you may not have a water hole or an elephant's trunk, but try an outdoor garden sprinkler for older toddlers who are steady on their feet. Running through the water can be exciting, but cold and scary. Choose a sprinkler that sprays water low to the ground and not so forcefully that it frightens your child.

WHAT THEY LEARN. Simple games in the tub build positive and playful connections to the routines of good hygiene. It's a great time for one-on-one time with no interruptions for phones or other distractions. It's also a perfect time for using words that describe the water and how it feels, pours, and squirts.

Read It!

Jamberry

(by Bruce Degen, HarperCollins) A totally delicious nonsense rhyme about every kind of berry in the world. The playful lilt of the rhyme and rhythm make this a delight to recite; it will soon be chanted by young listeners. Enjoy the book as it is written and then go back and look at the action adventure of the little bear. There's so much to talk about as he romps through cascades of berries.

Play It!

Tasting Party · Language/kitchen science/concepts

During berry season, make a point of bringing home different kinds of berries from the supermarket or local fruit stand. Have a tasting party like the little bear. Recall some of the playful language of *Jamberry* as you are washing the berries together. Toddlers will like helping serve the berries on their cereal or in a dish. Have a comparison test with two kinds of berries. Talk about the taste, color and texture of the berries. Which are sweeter? Smoother? More sour?

Winterberries

You may not be able to buy fresh berries in the winter, but why not have a berry tasting jam party for breakfast or an afternoon treat? Store-bought sugarless and low-sugar jams are good treats on toast or crackers. Invite all teddy bears to the feast!

No-Cook Smashberry Jamberry Jam

Toddlers will love having a hand in smashing the berries and pouring in the sugar and other ingredients needed for this simple no-cook recipe. You can keep this for three weeks in the refrigerator or store it in your freezer.

One cup of strawberries
Half a cup of raspberries
Two-and-a-half cups of sugar
One tablespoon of lemon juice
One pouch of liquid fruit pectin

Step 1. Use a potato masher to smash the berries in a large bowl.

Step 2. Add sugar and mix well. Allow it to stand 10–15 minutes.

Step 3. Combine lemon juice and pectin. Stir into fruit. Stir for 3–4 minutes.

Step 4. Spoon mix into plastic containers and cover with lids.

Step 5. Keep at room temperature until it sets. May take a full day.

Step 6. Store in refrigerator up to three weeks or in freezer for longer.

WHAT THEY LEARN. So much of the food we eat comes "ready-made" from packages and jars. Making jam from scratch helps children see how the berries are transformed from solid to liquid and back to semi-solid again.

Read It!

Bear Snores On

(by Karma Wilson/illus. by Jane Chapman, Little Simon) Told in lilting verse, this cumulative tale begins with a sleeping bear whose cave is visited by one small animal after another. It's a stormy night and as the animals arrive they have a wonderful party . . . but Bear snores on! Little listeners will love repeating the refrain and enjoy the full circle that this charming tale takes as Bear awakes and his friends snore on! There's nothing scary here, just a soothing, snuggle-time story. Available in Spanish.

Play It!

Picnic Time

After reading *Bear Snores On*, it's fun to have a picnic—even if it is winter and too cold to eat outdoors. Make some easy snacks together. Invite your toddler's favorite teddy bear. Put Teddy in a snug place and let the bear snore on.

Recipes for Indoor Picnic:

Crunchy Munchies

Your toddler can help you mix this special treat
- One scoop of raisins
- Two scoops of Cheerios
- Three scoops of little pretzels

Mix well and listen as you munch. Is it crunchy enough to hear?
Listen again. What other sounds can you hear if you are very quiet?

Gram-Jam Bear Crackers

Give your older toddler a butter spreader to help you spread jam on graham crackers to make Gram-Jam Bear Cracker sandwiches for the picnic.

Play It Again   **Dramatic Play**

This is just a silly game that calls for lots of giggling and tickling. Pretend that you are the bear in the story and close your eyes and do some snoring. Toddlers will enjoy trying to wake you. Keep snoring and turn gently from side to side. You'll know when the joke is running out. At that time wake up and tickle the tots. No growling or scaring allowed! This is supposed to be fun! Older toddlers will enjoy taking turns playing the bear. By all means, ham it up and act scared until they tickle you!

You can also make a cave with a sheet draped over several chairs. Toddlers love going inside cozy places.

WHAT THEY LEARN. The big idea here is that one story can inspire children to replay and expand on an idea in many different ways.

Read It! Play It! with Babies and Toddlers is also available in Spanish: ¡A leer y jugar! con bebés y niños pequeños. ISBN: 0-972105050

Visit our website.

www.toyportfolio.com Updates, reviews of award winners, media listings, and parenting articles.

Are you in a parenting group or play group?

Contact us about special rates available for fundraisers and bulk orders.

Oppenheim Toy Portfolio, Inc.
40 East 9th St., Suite 14M
New York, New York 10003
(212) 598-0502
www.toyportfolio.com

About the Oppenheims

Founded in 1989, the **Oppenheim Toy Portfolio** is the only independent review of children's media. **Joanne Oppenheim** is one of the country's leading experts on children's literature, play, and development. She was honored with the Curious George Foundation Award for her work promoting literacy. Her daughter, **Stephanie Oppenheim,** is a child development expert and former corporate lawyer. She co-founded the Oppenheim Toy Portfolio with her mother soon after her first son was born. Long before she started reviewing children's books with her mother, she always enjoyed hearing her mother read to her! Joanne and Stephanie are contributors to NBC's Today show. Both live in New York City.